THE RF-101 VOODOO
OVER
SOUTH EAST ASIA
1961 - 1970

by

William H. Greenhalgh

DEFENSE
LION
PUBLICATIONS

Acknowledgements

This study was prepared by William H. Greenhalgh, historian on the staff of the Albert F. Simpson Historical Research Center, Maxwell Air Force Base, Alabama. Designated AFSHRC Historical Study No. 149, this historically documented analysis is one of a continuing series in progress at the center.

Abstract

Conceived in the final months of World War II as the XF-88, the McDonnell F-101 Voodoo came into being 12 years later as a supersonic, single-place, twin-engined tactical fighter. Its reconnaissance version, the RF-101A, first joined Tactical Air Command reconnaissance squadrons at Shaw Air Force Base in March 1957, and two years later PACAF's two reconnaissance squadrons converted to the stronger RF-l01C Voodoo. When first assigned to PACAF, the RF-101C carried a nose oblique camera and a three-camera fan array ahead of the cockpit, a viewfinder that allowed the pilot to see the ground below and ahead of his aircraft, and a split-vertical arrangement of two large-format cameras behind the cockpit. Subsequent modifications installed faster cameras for low-altitude missions and improved controls, but also introduced the unpopular small-format cameras. With two 15,000-pound-thrust jet engines with afterburners, it had a speed of 875 knots, and its 3,150 gallons of JP-4 fuel gave it a combat radius of more than 800 miles. It was light on the controls and highly maneuverable.

Among the first U.S. reconnaissance aircraft in Southeast Asia, the RF-101Cs from PACAF's squadrons spent long periods of temporary duty at Don Muang Airport and Udorn Royal Thai Air Force Base in Thailand and at Tan Son Nhut Air Base, South Vietnam, photographing vital objectives in Laos and South Vietnam to provide most of the intelligence used by U.S. and South Vietnamese forces. Using a photoflash cartridge pod designed for another type of aircraft, the Voodoo pilots also developed a limited night photographic capability. When the United States finally decided to bomb targets in North Vietnam, RF-101C pilots took the first prestrike and poststrike photographs and led the Air Force and Vietnamese strike aircraft to the targets. The Voodoo pilots photographed objectives all the way to the China border, surviving anti-aircraft fire, missiles, and MiG interceptors – and suffering losses. Production of the RF-101s had halted well before hostilities began in Southeast Asia and combat losses rapidly reduced the number of aircraft available, causing the Air Force to concentrate all remaining Voodoos in one squadron at Tan Son Nhut Air Base. As age and combat continued to take their toll, even those Voodoos were withdrawn in November 1970, terminating the long saga of the McDonnell RF-101C.

Copyright

ORIGINAL FOREWORD

It is impossible to separate an aircraft from its pilots and support personnel since they constitute a team. Nor is it possible to describe that team without considering the organizational and operational developments which affected the team's performance. This volume is a narrative of the birth and growth of the RF-101C Voodoo, its entry into the conflict in Southeast Asia, the growth of the reconnaissance force, the problems encountered and the factors which eventually forced its withdrawal from combat.

This study has been prepared by William H. Greenhalgh, historian on the staff of the Albert F. Simpson Historical Research Center, Maxwell Air Force Base, Alabama. Designated AFSHRC Historical Study No. 149, this historically documented analysis is one of a continuing series in progress at the Center.

JOHN W. HUSTON

Major General, USAF
Chief, Office of Air Force History

FOREWORD
By Defense Lion Publications

The last McDonnell F-101 Voodoo was withdrawn from service almost exactly 40 years ago. Today, the F-101 family of aircraft is almost forgotten except to the community of aircraft enthusiasts and the smaller community of those who flew this aircraft. Designed as a long-range escort fighter for the heavy bombers of Strategic Air Command, it was obsolescent in this role before the first prototypes flew. Instead it served as a tactical fighter, a home-defense interceptor, and a reconnaissance aircraft. In the last of these roles, the RF-101C proved to be a versatile and valuable aircraft that carried out exceptionally hazardous duties over North Vietnam. In doing so, the RF-101 fleet was essentially expended, with many being shot down, lost in accidents, or simply worn out by the demands of strenuous wartime service.

In a larger sense, the importance of reconnaissance aircraft is often overlooked. There have been multiple accounts of the operations conducted by various types of fighter and bomber aircraft, ranging from AD-1 Skyraiders to B-52 Stratofortresses, but for these to do their work, the targets had to be found and identified. This history highlights just how vital – and how dangerous – the role of reconnaissance aircraft was. After the attack aircraft had done their work, the reconnaissance aircraft had to return to the target and determine how much damage had been done. The Vietnamese anti-aircraft gunners were well aware of the importance of bomb damage assessment and knew that, after the American strike was over, an RF-101 would soon be flying overhead. Truly, the pilots of the RF-101s had a deadly dangerous job, and this history of their achievements pays a much-deserved tribute to their skill and fortitude.

This book was originally written in March 1979 and was approved for public release in 2006. This compilation consists of the original text in full, supplemented by additional material that has become available in recent years. When the original monograph was written, the F-101 was still in service and some of its performance details were classified. This has now changed, and new material has allowed a more rounded picture of the aircraft's capabilities to be presented. The primary changes are to the first chapter dealing with the development of the F-101 and its introduction to service. This has been greatly expanded with the addition of new material that has become available over the last 30 years. We have also added a final chapter that discusses the post-Vietnam War history of the RF-101 fleet and attempts to find a successor. With these exceptions, the integrity of the original text has been scrupulously maintained.

Other changes are cosmetic in nature. Over the passage of time the original documents had been stained, damaged, annotated, copied and recopied. These defects have been removed and the manuscript electronically cleaned. Unfortunately, over the passage of time and repeated copying, the pictures in the original have become badly degraded and are barely legible. In some cases we were able to hunt down examples of the original pictures and replace the damaged copies with new scans of those illustrations. In others, the pictures had to be replaced by ones of similar content.

One of the changes we made also reflects the passage of time since the original monograph was written. Back then, the names of Southeast Asian battlegrounds, and especially those in Vietnam, were part of the language. It was well-known that casual mention of "going downtown" meant flying into the Hanoi/Haiphong area, a location protected by the heaviest air defenses in the world. Now, those names have faded into history. As a result, we have included a number of maps to help readers orient themselves to the geography of a war that ended 40 years ago. We have also inserted numerous new photographs that help illustrate the activities of the RF-101C fleet and the environment in which they flew.

CONTENTS

ILLUSTRATIONS

CHAPTER ONE
THE VOODOO

(This Chapter has been revised and enhanced by Defense Lion Publications)

The U.S. Air Force traditionally has modified fighter, bomber or transport aircraft to obtain its reconnaissance aircraft, and the McDonnell RF-101 Voodoo was no exception. Conceived in the final months of World War II, the RF-101 took 12 years to come to life and several more years to achieve the recognition it deserved. The Voodoo was not available for the Korea police action, but it was ready for the conflict in South-East Asia (SEA). One of the first tactical jet aircraft to take part in military operations over Laos and North Vietnam, it performed assigned tasks well. A day reconnaissance aircraft, it nevertheless functioned fairly well in all-weather conditions and eventually developed a limited night photographic capability. Its cameras produced photography from which the photo interpreters extracted much of the intelligence information necessary for bombing North Vietnam and planning military operations in Laos, Cambodia, and South Vietnam.

Development of the XF-88 Voodoo

The strategic bombing campaigns conducted by the USAAF during World War II had shown that bombing raids would suffer prohibitive casualties unless the bombers either had a marked performance advantage over enemy interceptors or were provided with a fighter escort that could protect them to and from their targets. During World War II, the B-29 achieved some level of protection under the first category by virtue of its high performance compared with most Japanese aircraft, while the P-51 Mustang provided an excellent long-range escort.

The USAAF had also realized that any technology development resulting in improved bomber performance could also be applied to fighters to increase their ability to make interceptions. Thus, there was likely to be a constant swing of advantage between fighters and bombers. The advent of the jet engine looked as if it would confer a major performance advantage to defensive fighters that would be of significant operational importance. This would need to be matched by equally advanced long-range escort fighters. Unfortunately, the engines used to power the first jet aircraft were notorious for their excessive fuel consumption, and lacked the range and endurance of their piston-engined counterparts. As a result, they would be unable to escort the B-29, B-50, and B-36 bombers all the way to their targets. It was therefore essential to produce a new, long-range jet fighter escort. A variety of concepts were evaluated, including fighters towed by the bombers or carried by them. More practical suggestions included mixed power concepts such as the Convair XP-81, which would cruise on its piston engine and use the jet only for combat. Another approach involved the construction of the Bell XP-83, a large, bulky fighter that was essentially a flying fuel tank. None of these early ideas proved practical, since the available engines did not give enough power to lift the fuel needed for the required range.

Despite the disappointing results of the first efforts to develop a long-range jet fighter, the USAAF tried again in early 1946. This time, a specific set of performance and range requirements were laid down for the new "penetration fighter." These stipulated a combat radius of at least 900 miles and a performance capable of meeting all opposing fighters on more than equal terms. In addition, the USAAF stipulated a maximum gross weight not to exceed 15,000 pounds. In view of the disappointing performance of the XP-81 and XP-83, these were onerous requirements.

Having manufactured parts and major components for a number of aircraft during World War II, the young McDonnell Aircraft Corporation of St. Louis, Missouri, joined the giants of the aircraft industry responding to this requirement. On April 1, 1946, they initiated work on the Model 36, a large twin-jet aircraft powered by a pair of 3,000-pound-thrust Westinghouse J34 engines. McDonnell Aircraft had already established a reputation for being ready to adopt innovative solutions in an effort to achieve high performance. The Model 36 showed that this reputation was deserved. The engines were fed by air intakes mounted in the wing roots, but the engines themselves were installed underneath the rear fuselage. This configuration was adopted to reduce drag while leaving enough space in the fuselage for the fuel needed for the long-range escort mission. The wings were swept back at 35 degrees. In view of the high expected speed of the aircraft, a V-tail was selected to reduce compressibility effects that were causing deep concern as aircraft speeds approached the sound barrier. A set of perforated dive brakes was mounted on the rear fuselage, hinged at the rear. The pilot's cockpit was situated well forward of the wing. The armament was to be six 20mm cannon.

A number of changes to this design were made as a result of mockup inspections and wind tunnel tests during the summer of 1946. These included giving the wing root intakes 40 degrees of sweep and a boundary layer ramp. The V-tail was found to cause stability problems and was replaced by conventional swept surfaces. The tailplane was, however, mounted partway up the fin to keep it in undisturbed airflow. Pleased by the way the new fighter was evolving, the USAAF confirmed an order for two prototypes on February 14, 1947. The first of these was delivered on August 11, 1948 and flew for the first time on October 20.

The flight test program went reasonably well given the rate at which the state-of-the-art was advancing during the late 1940s. Some minor problems were experienced, with the air intakes being unable to cope with the airflow required by the engines. Other problems were more traditional. The roll rate was inadequate and required significant stiffening of the wing structure. The dive brakes caused excessive buffeting, while the aircraft suffered from excessive yaw and roll characteristics in some flight regimes. Yet, once these problems were addressed, handling characteristics were generally satisfactory by the standards of the time.

It was the performance of the XF-88 that was disappointing. A combination of weight increases and the relatively low-powered engines resulted in a maximum speed significantly less than that predicted. Maximum speed at sea level was only 641 mph, some 40 mph slower than that of the F-86A Sabre, which was then just entering production. The rate of climb was also mush slower than anticipated, with the aircraft needing approximately six minutes to reach an altitude of 30,000 feet. As had been the case since the program was started, range was a problem. It simply could not be reached using any reasonable quantity of internal fuel and, to satisfy USAF range requirements, the 734-U.S.-gallon internal fuel capacity had to be supplemented by 350-gallon wingtip tanks. However, it quickly became apparent that serious aerodynamic problems would be encountered when these tip tanks were mounted.

The XF-88.
Source: U.S. Air Force

No matter how the problems with the XF-88 were addressed, the answer came out the same way. The aircraft had to have a lot more power. The easiest solution was to fit afterburners to the J34 engines. A more comprehensive solution would have been to replace the J34s with Westinghouse J46 afterburning turbojets that gave twice as much thrust. Funding considerations did not allow the J46 installation, but adapting the second prototype to carry afterburning J34 engines was possible. Using a McDonnell-devised afterburner boosted the thrust of each Westinghouse XJ34-WE-15 engine from 3,600 pounds to 4,825 pounds. The second prototype was also fitted with bladder fuel cells in the wings to increase internal fuel capacity to 834 gallons. In this configuration, the aircraft was designated the XF-88A. When it made its first flight on April 26, 1949, the improvement in performance was remarkable. Maximum speed at sea level was almost 700 mph, time to climb to 30,000 feet was cut to 4 minutes, and takeoff run was reduced by 20 percent.

Despite its new-found performance, the XF-88A lost out to the North American XF-93A, a highly modified version of the F-86 Sabre. In December 1948, McDonnell was instructed to stop design and development work on the F-88, but

9

was permitted to continue flight testing on the two prototypes. However, the tight financial environment meant that procurement of interceptors and strategic bombers took priority. By the time funding allowed production of the penetration fighter, the belief had grown that no production order for aircraft of this type should be awarded until a competitive fly-off between the contenders had been carried out. When that fly-off was conducted, the McDonnell XF-88A scored a decisive victory over its rivals and was selected for production.

The XF-88A was already evolving beyond the constraints of its original specifications. Air Force headquarters had asked the Air Materiel Command (AMC) to examine the possibility of converting the XF-88A to a reconnaissance aircraft with interchangeable nose sections to allow one airframe to function alternately as a fighter or reconnaissance aircraft. If the designer could devise both gun and reconnaissance noses that maintenance crews could inter change in the field, the XF-88A could become a truly versatile aircraft. Although the interchangeable nose idea proved unworkable, the work related to it showed that the XF-88As speed and long range gave it the potential to be an effective reconnaissance aircraft.

It was the Korean War that killed the XF-88. It is the iron law of mobilization that priority must be given to the procurement of existing types rather than a changeover to new types of equipment. So, although the outbreak of war in Korea opened the financial taps and funding flowed once again, the largesse was directed to the production of the existing F-84 and F-86. In addition, the development of long-range, high-speed jet bombers such as the B-47 and the B-52 appeared to eliminate any real need for penetration fighters. As the XF-88 project fell victim to the war effort, the interchangeable nose idea also died. [1]

A final legacy in the XF-88 saga was the use of the first XF-88 as the XF-88B propeller research vehicle, fitted with a 2,750-shp Allison XT38-A-5 turboprop in the nose. The XF-88B spent most of its time at the Langley Memorial Aeronautical Laboratory. Testing continued until 1956. It had the distinction of being the final propeller-driven fighter in the USAF designation series. Both the XF-88A and the XF-88B were eventually scrapped.

The XF-88B (the nose turboprop is feathered).
Source: U.S. Air Force

Development of the F-101 Voodoo

The Air Force assumption that the high performance of the B-47 and B-52 bombers would make escort fighters unnecessary in any future conflict was quickly challenged by the experiences of the Korean War. The streams of B-29 bombers attacking targets in North Korea were intercepted by Korean, Chinese and Russian MiG-15s that proved more than capable of shooting down the piston-engined bombers. Casualties in the bomb groups started to mount, and even the provision of Republic F-84 Thunderjet fighters proved to be of limited value. The performance of the F-84 was already dated, and the aircraft proved incapable of protecting the B-29s from the MiG-15s. A more capable U.S. fighter, the North American F-86 Sabre, was available, but it lacked the range and endurance to provide effective escort.

A Sudden Change in Opinions – A MiG-15 Captured by the U.S. Air Force.
Source: U.S. Air Force

Why this situation should have been so unanticipated is puzzling. The U.S. Air Force had long appreciated that there was a constant swing in balance between the capabilities of attacking bombers and defending fighters, and that any technology that pushed the balance in favor of one could always be exploited to return the balance in favor of the other. The B-29 was, by 1950, an obsolescent design already being replaced in Strategic Air Command frontline service. That was, after all, why it had been released for service in the Korean War. Even in 1945, the performance edge of the B-29 had been marginal: 74 B-29s had been lost to fighters, 54 to anti-aircraft fire, and 19 to a combination of the two. The MiG-15 was at least three generations more advanced than anything the Japanese had

11

operated and the B-29s suffered accordingly. By the end of the Korean War, 34 had been lost.

One reason why the question of fighter escorts had been neglected was the unanticipated ascendancy of the B-36. The B-36 operated at altitudes that prevented even the MiG-15 from engaging the aircraft effectively. Attempts to "intercept" B-36s using a captured MiG-15 showed that the Soviet-designed fighter could only just barely reach B-36 operational altitudes. If it attempted to engage the bombers, it would stall and spin out when it fired its guns. At those altitudes, the B-36 could actually outmaneuver opposition fighters. With the prospect of the B-47 and B-52 having much better performance than the B-36, the lack of any urgent need for an escort fighter must have appeared convincing.

There was another factor as well. The U.S. had no real operational experience of its own with interceptor fighters at this time. In World War II, its fighter inventory had consisted of tactical fighters intended to support the Army and long-range escorts intended to protect the heavy bombers. With the homeland protected by long stretches of ocean, there was no real need for interceptors prior to World War II. While a dedicated interceptor was a poor tactical support fighter and useless for long-range escort, it was more effective at its design role of shooting down bombers than the U.S. planners realized. Thus, the B-29 losses over Korea came as a much-needed wake-up call.

Absorbing the lessons from the appearance of the MiG-15 over Korea, Strategic Air Command returned to its original doctrine that performance advantages were transitory and that a much longer-range escort fighter that could fight contemporary interceptors on equal terms was needed. This meant building a fighter that had sufficient range and combat ceiling to accompany the Convair B-36 intercontinental bomber, adequate speed to escort the B-47 and B-52, and the air-to-air capability needed to engage the MiG-15 and its successors. In February 1951, the USAF issued a requirement for a fighter to fill this need.

Five companies submitted proposals to meet this requirement. These included Lockheed offering versions of the F-90 and the F-94, North American with an updated F-93, and Northrop suggesting an escort version of the F-89 Scorpion all-weather interceptor. Republic based its proposals on variants of the F-84. As its entry, McDonnell proposed a larger and more powerful version of its XF-88 penetration fighter prototype. McDonnell Aircraft Corporation redesigned the XF-88 to carry larger engines, lengthened the fuselage to provide additional fuel storage, and submitted its strategic fighter proposal. The new aircraft was the first Air Force fighter designed to be supersonic. The McDonnell submission was judged the winner of the competition in May 1951. In October of that year, the USAF reprogrammed FY52 funds previously allocated to the F-84F and F-86F program to get McDonnell's proposal into production right away. On November 30, 1951, the new and improved version of the F-88A was designated the F-101.

The Air Force was determined to avoid the problems of being underpowered that had plagued the F-88. The McDonnell team had recommended that the F-101 be powered by a pair of afterburning Allison J71 turbojets offering 10,200 pounds of thrust with afterburners. However, the Air Force believed that this was still inadequate and demanded McDonnell use a pair of Pratt & Whitney J57 afterburning engines offering 16,900 pounds of thrust with afterburner. These engines required a much greater air flow than the earlier proposals, requiring the air intakes in the wing roots be redesigned and considerably enlarged. The fuel-thirsty engines needed considerably more fuel and this demanded that the fuselage be lengthened and widened to triple the internal fuel capacity from 734 gallons to 2,341 U.S. gallons. Provisions were made for a pair of 450-gallon external tanks.

The Air Research and Development Command (ARDC) in June 1952 asked the Wright Air Development Center (WADC) to determine whether interchangeable noses could permit the F-101 to operate alternately as a reconnaissance aircraft and a fighter. This would offer a useful additional capability to that provided by the RB-36 and RB-47. Two factors seemed to preclude such versatility. First, the layout of a reconnaissance cockpit differed from that of a fighter aircraft, and any combination of the two would be overcomplicated. Further, a reconnaissance nose to hold the 36-inch focal length KA-1 cameras would be so big that it would unbalance the whole airframe and interfere with the air intakes. A 29-foot interchangeable nose and cockpit section was considered briefly, but its length would have created new problems.[2]

When the Korean War ended, a more measured assessment of the threat was made. This highlighted several factors that had previously been overlooked. The most important was that the B-29 raids over Korea had essentially been World War II-style bombing missions conducted by relatively large formations of bombers dropping masses of conventional bombs. The strategic offensive against the Soviet Union would be an entirely different type of operation, with the bombers proceeding to their targets independently and dropping nuclear weapons on those objectives. A traditional fighter escort was impossible; instead, the "escort" mission would consist of delivering nuclear weapons to enemy airbases and air defense installations, causing diversions, and fighting off enemy interceptors. Accordingly, Strategic Air Command wanted McDonnell to redesign the F-101 to carry out this type of strategic penetration and nuclear strike mission.

A further reconsideration of the new mission profile suggested that the range of the F-101A was nowhere near enough to be able to escort SAC's bombers all the way to the target. The mission would instead be assigned to medium bombers, especially the upcoming B-58 Hustler. Consequently, the Strategic Air Command lost any interest in the F-101 as an escort fighter. In its place, Tactical Air Command (TAC) saw the potential of the aircraft as a nuclear-armed fighter-bomber and requested that the F-101A be acquired by the command. The TAC version of the F-101A was armed with four 20mm cannon and could carry a single 1,620-pound or 3,271-pound "special store," – i.e., a nuclear bomb. The F-101As were equipped with the MA-7 fire control system as well as with the LABS (Low-Altitude Bombing System) for toss-release of their nuclear bombs. The F-101A could not carry or deliver conventional bombs.

As part of the shift from SAC to TAC, ARDC on 17 October, 1953 published its requirements for a reconnaissance version of the F-l0lA, but made no mention of interchangeable noses. It asked for a reconnaissance aircraft capable of both day and night photography, carrying the same navigation system as the F-101, an ultra high frequency (UHF) command radio set, and a chaff dispenser. The aircraft would carry no armament.[3]

Personnel from Air Force headquarters, ARDC, and AMC conferred on 4 December 1952 and on 27 January 1953 to select the cameras, viewfinder, electronic equipment, and other specialized subsystems for the RF-101. They asked the builder to stow the photoflash cartridges internally, if possible, to eliminate the need for external ejector pods. They also had learned that McDonnell Aircraft Corporation had developed for the Navy's F2H-2F a lighter and less expensive camera control system capable of handling more cameras than the RF-101 would carry, and asked that the builder consider using it in the RF-101. In April, the Air Force asked that the designers add a radar altimeter to the RF-l0l equipment, and a month later asked them to delete the 600-pound AN/APN-82 electronic navigation system, leaving only a ground position indicator and a manual course-and-distance computer.[4]

As the design work neared completion, the Air Force in July 1953 asked McDonnell Aircraft Corporation to quote a firm price for two YRF-101A's, 28 RF-101A's, and 56 F-101A's, delivery to begin in June 1955. Two months later (September 1953), the Air Force issued a Fiscal Year (FY) 1954 procurement directive for 86 F-101 aircraft and received McDonnell's price and delivery proposal. AMC on 10 November authorized McDonnell to modify two F-l01A's into YRF-101A's to satisfy the FY 1954 procurement plan, and in June 1954 amended the contract to cover the changed production schedule.[5]

Under the terms of this amendment, the 16th and 17th F-101A airframes were set aside for conversion to unarmed photographic reconnaissance configuration. They retained the J57-P-13 engines of the fighter-bomber version but had a redesigned and longer nose housing four cameras designed for low-altitude photography. Because of the size of the KA-l cameras, one of the designer's greatest problems had been the requirement to carry all cameras in the nose. The project office finally permitted the designers to move the KA-l split-vertical cameras to the rear of the cockpit where the deeper fuselage could accommodate their bulk. The dual-mode inflight refueling system of the fighter version was retained, but the internal fuel tank arrangement was revised slightly resulting in a slightly reduced fuel capacity of 2250 gallons. ARDC also specified that the contractor install the universal camera control system because it believed the newer Navy system to be "too experimental." AMC approved the new configuration on 13 January 1954.[6]

As approved, the RF-101A was slightly longer and much sleeker than the F-l0lA. The reconnaissance nose held four cameras and a viewfinder, while the two 36-inch focal length KA-l cameras had a separate bay behind the pilot, but ahead of the fuel tanks. The RF-101 also carried a UHF command radio; a direction finder; an identification, friend or foe (IFF) set; an omni-range navigation receiver; a ground position indicator; and a radar altimeter. Because there was no room in the airframe, the designers made no provision for internal stowage of photoflash cartridges or ejectors, and the RF-l0l became a day reconnaissance aircraft.[7]

14

Faced with rapidly shrinking funds, the Air Force on 16 April 1954 issued a production stop order for all aircraft being procured for FY 1954. Work remained at a standstill until 2 November 1954, when AMC told McDonnell to resume production. The first YRF-101 rolled off the production line in May 1955 and flew for the first time during the week of 3 July. [8]

Inevitably, the transfer from SAC to TAC spawned other aircraft configuration changes, such as TAC's request for five more pieces of electronic equipment to establish an air-to-ground communications capability for tactical missions. The contractor was forced to make structural changes to aircraft under construction, and to plan further alterations for airframes not yet begun. TAC finally provided its operational concept of RF-l01 employment in July 1956, and on 8 August, AMC told the McDonnell Aircraft Corporation to make further changes in the RF-101 airframe to meet TAC's requirements. Among the more significant changes was a TAC decision that the RF-l0l carry two external pods loaded with electronic countermeasures (ECM) equipment, the standard fighter ECM pods developed by North American Aviation. [9]

Due to shortages of the camera equipment needed for the new aircraft, many of these early RF-101As were initially delivered without a full set of cameras, which severely limited their picture-taking capability. Gradually, however, this equipment was eventually delivered and installed and the RF-101As were finally made fully capable of carrying out their primary missions.

As a result of the many design changes and equipment additions, the contractor gradually had strengthened the aircraft and increased its capability. The first F-101A's and RF-101A's were designed with a maneuvering load factor of 6.33 times the force of gravity (G), but later aircraft were built to a 7.33 factor. Because the F-101B designation already had been assigned to a two-place interceptor version of the Voodoo designed for the Air Defense Command (ADC), the project office in June 1956 recommended that the Air Force redesignate RF-l0lA's numbered 56-162 through 56-231 as RF-101Cs to show that they were built to the higher G strength factor. Three months later, the Air Force made the redesignation official. [10] Various additional contract charges raised the total production to 203 by January 1959.

McDonnell had completed production of 203 RF-101's by January 1959, including two YRF-101 prototypes and four RF-l0lA's for Nationalist China under the Military Assistance Program (MAP). During the test phase, a number of systems and individual parts had failed -- primarily in the autopilot, hydraulic system, viewfinder, and control system actuating cylinders. The contractor promptly corrected each fault, and replaced defective parts with better designed items. [11] However, the pilots flying them in England did not like them. When flying in the landing pattern at 170-180 knots, the aircraft had a tendency to pitch up if there was a big gust or a quick movement on the stick. Once it pitched, the tail would blank out the horizontal stabilizer and the only way to get the nose down was to pop the drag chute. The aircraft had a warning light and a stick shaker to warn the pilots when they were getting close to the critical speed. The pilots claimed they would be flying on instruments in landing configuration with the light and the stick shaker going.

Air Force headquarters on 22 March 1957 announced that it had assigned RF-101A's to an operational wing at Shaw Air Force Base,[12] and as quickly as RF-101's came off the production line in St. Louis, Air Force headquarters assigned them to one of nine tactical reconnaissance squadrons. In addition to three squadrons at Shaw Air Force Base and four in France, Pacific Air Forces (PACAF) scheduled its 15th Tactical Reconnaissance Squadron at Kadena Air Base, Okinawa, and the 45th Tactical Reconnaissance Squadron at Misawa Air Base, Japan, to convert from RF-84F's to RF-101Cs. The 15th Tactical Reconnaissance Squadron completed its conversion and became operational with the new aircraft in January 1959, and the 45th Tactical Reconnaissance Squadron followed 2 months later. The RF-101C was the only modern Air Force tactical reconnaissance aircraft in the western Pacific in 1959. [13]

In 1962, most RF-101s were fitted with new high resolution KA-45 cameras in the forward station and with two 12-inch KA-47s replacing the KA-1s. The aircraft were modified to allowed them to take photographs at lower altitudes. The installation of a centerline ejector pod with flash cartridges gave the RF-101 a limited night photography capability. The RF-101Cs were also fitted with a single hard point under the fuselage capable of carrying a nuclear weapon so that it could carry out a secondary nuclear strike mission if ever called upon to do so. A total of 166 RF-101Cs were built. They were the last single-seat Voodoos to be built for the USAF.

The original plan had been for the RF-101C to be gradually phased out of USAF service in favor of the McDonnell RF-4C Phantom II from 1965. As the RF-4Cs arrived, the RF-101Cs were to be transferred to the Air National Guard. However, the requirements of the Vietnam War forced the USAF to change its plans, and the RF-101C would continue in service much longer than originally intended. The Air National Guard did not get its first batch of RF-101Cs until early 1969. By then the aircraft were worn out, and they were retired from service in 1975.

The RF-101A Voodoo.
Source: U.S. Air Force

16

The RF-101C Voodoo. Source: U.S. Air Force

Voodoo Making a Typical Late 1950s Landing. Source: U.S. Air Force

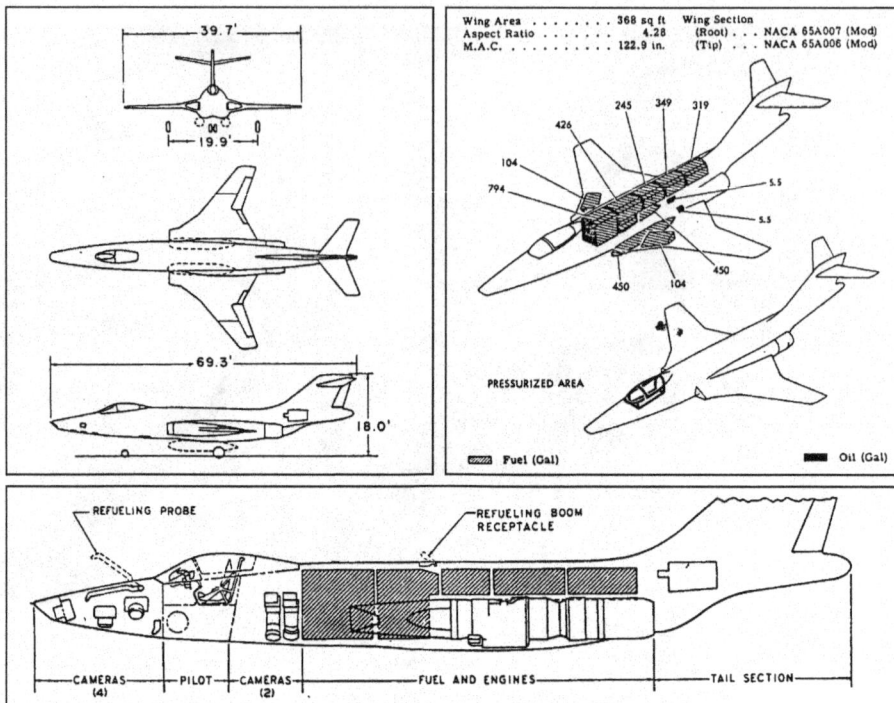

RF-101 Layout.

*For Remaining Pages of the RF-101 Standard Aircraft Characteristics Document,
See Appendix II*

The Reconnaissance Voodoo

A single-place, twin-jet aircraft with sweptback wings and tail surfaces, the RF-101C was powered by two Pratt and Whitney J-57-P-13 engines, rated at 15,000 pounds of thrust each with afterburner, which gave it a combat speed of 875 knots in basic mission configuration. Even under full power without after-burner (i.e., military power), it had an exceptional rate of climb and was highly maneuverable. Its physical characteristics are shown below:

Wing Span	39.7 feet
Length	69.3 feet
Height	18.0 feet
Weight - Empty	26,136 pounds
- Combat.	36,586 pounds
- Takeoff	48,133 pounds
Fuel (JP-4)	3,150 gallons

It carried its 20,475 pounds of JP-4 fuel in fuselage and wing tanks and in two 450-gallon external drop tanks. It had a retractable refueling probe recessed into the forward fuselage and a refueling receptacle atop the fuselage aft of the cockpit, making possible aerial refueling with either the probe-and-drogue or the flying boom method.[14]

The designers put the two engines in the bottom of the fuselage to improve access for maintenance and installed speed brakes and a drag chute in the aft portion. The cockpit had 5.0 pounds per square inch (psi) differential pressurization, pressure suit connections, an oxygen system, air-conditioning and heating and an ejection seat. The nose gear was steerable, and a hydraulic system operated the tricycle landing gear and the flight controls.[15]

Some pilots thought the MB-1 autopilot reacted too abruptly to changes in orientation, but worked well at altitudes from 500 to 42,000 feet. Because the Air Force had eliminated the planned AN/APN-82 electronic navigation system, the aircraft had very limited all-weather capability. The AN/ASN-6 automatic navigation computer did not provide sufficient data to assist the pilot, and the AN/ARN-14 omni-range receiver was useful only over friendly territory where range stations were available. The ARA-25 direction finder worked well on clear channels, but the pilots considered it unreliable in areas of high signal density. The drift computer built into the viewfinder was usable only in visual flight rules (VFR) weather, and even then was seldom more accurate than forecast winds. Navigation accuracy depended almost entirely upon the skill and ingenuity of the pilot.

Maintenance personnel liked its easily removed panels that provided quick access to 95 percent of the components that normally required base-level maintenance, and claimed that the RF-101C was much easier to maintain than the RF-84F it replaced. Operations people said it was a good weapon system and the pilots liked the way it handled.[16] Only 4 pounds of force and a very slight stick movement sufficed for takeoff, a sharp contrast to the high stick forces and full rearward stick displacement needed for the RF-84F. Takeoff usually was accomplished without afterburner because normal power provided excellent acceleration and good climb speed. Most pilots felt at ease in the RF-101, a responsive and stable aircraft with excellent cockpit visibility. Although tests indicated that it was not as stable a camera platform as the RF-84F, it produced excellent photography.[17]

Because tactical reconnaissance missions required frequent and rapid altitude changes, the resulting extremes of temperature forced the designers to provide insulation, heat, cooling, and dehumidified air for all camera bays. A relatively stable temperature and dry air were necessary to prevent expansion and contraction of lens cones, which could cause out-of-focus photography, and to avoid moisture condensation on the cameras and camera windows. To prevent fogging of the latter, the Air Force specified that the camera windows be specially coated and heated. The coating reduced light transmission properties of the glass by almost 20 percent, causing serious film under exposure until an adjustment in the LA-15 computer power supply compensated for the light loss. It also was necessary to double the filter factor on the oblique cameras to compensate for the coating. Heater filaments in the camera windows never were connected, but apparently caused some image degradation by reflecting extraneous light into the camera lenses.[18]

The RF-l0l Cameras

Although the Air Force had selected for the RF-101 only those cameras considered best for the assigned mission, they began experimenting with new cameras almost at once. Throughout the life of the RF-l0.|, its camera configuration underwent almost continuous modification to improve the existing sensors or to try new ones. The results were not always good, but each change taught the Air Force. An examination of the original cameras, controls, and accessories provides a sound basis for understanding later changes and improvements.

Most Air Force aerial cameras in 1959 consisted of a lens cone, body, and film magazine or cassette. The body usually contained electrical connections, heaters, motors, and gears for driving the magazines, and mechanisms for winding and tripping the shutters. The lens cone held the lens at the precise focal distance from the film plane, and in most cameras also housed the shutter and diaphragm. The film magazine contained supply and take-up spools for the film, a film plane, and some mechanism for insuring that the film was in the proper position at the instant of exposure. In film magazines with image motion compensation, a drive mechanism moved the film at the instant of exposure to synchronize exactly with ground image movement. For the RF-101C, the Air Force had chosen framing cameras that produced a square or rectangular negative with each instantaneous exposure. The framing cameras in the RF-101C had interchangeable lens cones which permitted the substitution of different focal length lenses to adapt the cameras to changing requirements and circumstances. Later panoramic cameras wound the film past a slit during exposure as a synchronized lens or prism moved to change the image.

For the small nose compartment of the RF-101C, the Air Force chose a 12-inch focal length KA-2 framing camera for forward oblique photography on "dicing" missions--flown at extremely low altitudes for the specific purpose of obtaining nose or side oblique photographs. The camera featured a Rapidyne between-the-lens shutter with high shutter speeds and remotely adjustable shutter speed and lens aperture. The KA-2's standard or image motion compensation (IMC) magazines with recycle times of 1.75 or 0.6 seconds respectively, produced 9-inch square negatives. The nose camera produced particularly spectacular photography at low altitudes with high aircraft speeds.

A larger camera compartment just ahead of the cockpit contained 6-inch focal. length KA-2 cameras in a fan array of a vertical, left oblique, and right oblique. Basically, the same cameras as the nose camera but with shorter lens cones, the three KA-2's photographed a side-to-side swath from horizon to horizon with overlap between the three negatives. Unfortunately, when the pilot used the three cameras with A-9B standard magazines and a full load of 390 feet of film at low altitudes and high aircraft speeds, the short recycle time caused the drive motors to shear gears. When the recycle time was long enough, however, or when the film load was cut in half, the cameras operated effectively and produced excellent photography at almost any altitude or speed. Three KA-46 cameras could replace the KA-2 cameras for night photography if some means were devised to carry and eject the photoflash cartridges. The second compartment offered the greatest potential for arranging modifications of the camera system, providing plenty of room for the installation of larger cameras and infra-red, radar, and laser equipment. [19]

In the compartment behind the pilot, two KA-1 cameras were mounted as split verticals, each camera set slightly off-vertical so the two images overlapped in the center and covered about 28 degrees each side of the optical centerline. The mounts could accommodate either 24-inch or 36-inch lens cones, and the 9-inch by 18-inch KA-1 negatives were popular with the photo interpreters and Army users. The cameras proved effective at high speeds and low altitudes on day reconnaissance missions, particularly when using the A-28 IMC magazines.[20]

A viewfinder provided the pilot a look at the ground below and forward. At altitudes less than 5,000 feet, an attached LA-19 image velocity detector computed the velocity/height ratio and fed it to the camera control system, which then compensated for focal length and camera depression angle to establish the image motion compensation rate and exposure interval. The B-2 terrain light detector fed ground illumination data into the control system where preset film speed ratings and filter factors determined the proper apertures to be automatically set into each camera. In addition, the pilot could use the LA-21 master control to set exposure intervals or lens aperture. Under normal conditions the simplified camera control system (SCCS) provided virtually automatic operation, determining and setting proper exposure negative overlap, and image motion compensation.[21]

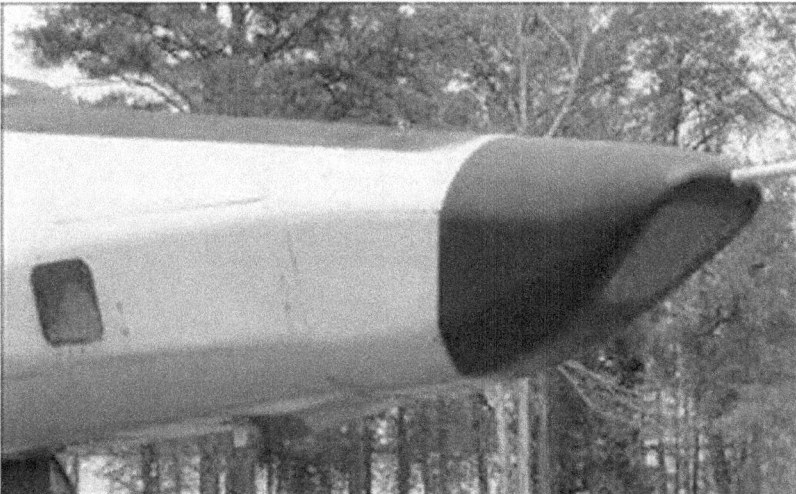

Close-up of the RF-101C nose section showing camera installations.
Source: U.S. Air Force

21

Film Being Unloaded From Cameras on an RF-101C. Source: U.S. Air Force

RF-101C at Than Son Nhut Air Base in South Vietnam. Source U.S. Air Force

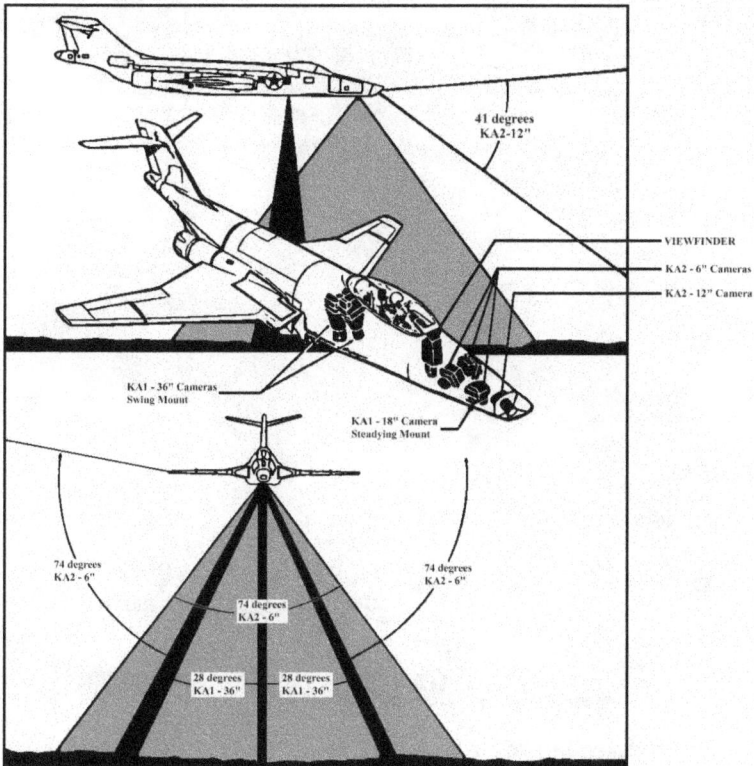

RF-101C Camera Coverage. Redrawn from U.S. Air Force Original.

Station	Camera	Focal Length (Inches)	Depression Angle (Degrees)	Camera Position	Camera Type	Image Size (Inches)
1	KS-72	6	15	Forward oblique	Frame	4.5 X 4.5
	KS-72	12	10	Forward oblique	Frame	
2	KA-56	3	-		Panoramic	
	*KA-18	3,6	-	Vertical stereo	Panoramic	4.5 X 9.75
	KA-18	6	-	Vertical strip	Strip	4.5 -
	*T-11	6	-	Precise mapping	Strip	9 -
	KS-72	3,6,12	-	Vertical	Frame	
	KS-72	6	72	Split vertical	Frame	4.5 X 4.5
	KS-72	6	37.5,25	Oblique	Frame	4.5 X 4.5
	KS-72	3	30	Oblique	Frame	4.5 X 4.5
	KS-72	12	5,15,25	Oblique (L or R only)	Frame	4.5 X 4.5
	KA-2	24	8,15,20	Oblique (L or R only)	Frame	9 X 9
3	KA-1	36	77	Split vertical	Frame	9 X 18
	KA-1	36	-	Vertical	Frame	

*Left and right camera station cannot be used when torquer stabilized mount is installed for the KA-18A or T-11.

RF-101 Aerial Camera Configurations. Source: U.S. Air Force

Port Casilda taken in 1962 during the Cuban Missile Crisis. The shadow of the RF-101 taking the picture can be seen in the bottom left hand corner.

Source: U.S. Air Force

Because the RF-101C was unarmed, the Air Force gave it the best passive defense equipment produced. An AN/APS-54 set gave an audio and visual warning of radar signals. Supposedly capable of determining whether the radar was ahead of or behind the RF-101C and whether the signal was of the sweep or lock-on type, the set allowed the pilot to make a quick threat analysis and take appropriate evasive action. Unfortunately the test pilots found the set quite worthless because in the test environment, the light and audio signals activated almost constantly, making bona fide signal recognition impossible.[22]

As initially configured, the RF-101 was a marginally effective day reconnaissance aircraft with many shortcomings but considerable promise. It was fast and maneuverable, but its photographic system needed improvement. Its camera bays were large enough to accommodate better cameras and other types of sensors, a potential misused on more than one occasion. The Voodoo attained operational status in the western Pacific with a limited capability and a mediocre reputation, but it was the most modern tactical reconnaissance aircraft in the Air Force.

CHAPTER II
VOODOOS IN SOUTHEAST ASIA

In 1959, PACAF converted two tactical reconnaissance squadrons in the western Pacific to RF-l0lC Voodoo aircraft. With world attention centered on the power struggle between the Communist and Western nations and military planning oriented toward all-out nuclear warfare, the Voodoos landed on the rim of a region that soon became the arena for the next military conflict involving U. S. forces.

Southeast Asia

Southeast Asia (SEA) in 1959 was of secondary concern to most of the world, even though an independence movement had been developing for several years. France had surrendered its control over Laos, Cambodia, and Vietnam, a region most familiar to the average American as Indochina. Neighboring Thailand, the storied Siam, was fiercely independent, a land of temples, elephants and exotic landscapes. It was all distant, indistinct, and unimportant in the eyes of most Americans. Unfortunately, the simmering political struggle in SEA would soon draw the United States into a conflict that would tear at the very fiber of American society. U.S. diplomats and military planners were concerned that they might not recognize new danger signals from the area because they had so little current information about SEA. Because aerial reconnaissance alone could solve many of the riddles, it became one of the first intelligence collection methods used.

An understanding of the geography and climate is essential to any evaluation of the problems and accomplishments of the RF-101C Voodoo in SEA. As used herein, the term SEA includes Laos, Vietnam, Cambodia, and Thailand, a mountainous peninsula jutting southward from the corner of the Asian land mass. Three rivers--the Red in the northeast, the Mekong in the center and south, and the Chao Phraya in Thailand—simultaneously divide and unite the region, providing inexpensive water transportation but impeding overland travel. Their deltas, particularly that of the Mekong, produce enough food in normal times to provide a surplus for export. Vegetation in SEA varies from open savannah to dense tropical rain forest with trees as tall as 200 feet and double or triple tree canopies. The jungle provides ideal cover for ground activity and makes aerial observation extremely difficult.

High temperatures and humidity throughout the year characterize the monsoon climate of the region. Twice each year, the prevailing winds reverse direction, producing dry and rainy seasons of roughly equal lengths. Along the east coast, the rainy weather includes long periods of low clouds, fog, and constant drizzle-- known locally as crachin weather--which inhibit or halt aerial reconnaissance operations. Pacific typhoons occasionally strike the Vietnamese coast, creating several days of poor weather before they lose their strength or head back out to sea. Burning rice fields and natural forest fires cause dense haze over much of the peninsula for several weeks each year, again inhibiting aerial reconnaissance over much of Laos and North Vietnam. [1]

South East Asia As It Was In 1960.
Source U.S. Air Force

The Growth of Conflict

Nationalist sentiment grew in Vietnam during World War II, nourished by strong anti-Japanese feeling and the removal of French control. Ho Chi Minh, a Nationalist as well as a Communist, led the independence movement that continued after the French returned. Although they granted limited independence within the French Union to Laos and Cambodia, the French maintained close control over Vietnam. When Ho's General Vo Nguyen Giap defeated the French force at remote Dien Bien Phu, the struggle entered a new phase.

Split into two parts by the 1954 Geneva agreements, Vietnam continued to experience terror and suffering as North Vietnam launched a campaign to subvert South Vietnam's independence and interfere with the internal politics of Laos. By 1959, the insurgent Viet Cong were increasingly active in South Vietnam; Pathet Lao and North Vietnamese forces threatened the Royal Laotian Government, and neutral Cambodia leaned toward closer relations with North Vietnam. The International Control Commission (ICC), established by the Geneva Agreements to monitor flare-ups and report violations, failed to censure the Communist aggression.

Aerial Reconnaissance

Laos first bore the brunt of North Vietnamese aggression as Pathet Lao and North Vietnamese troops seized two northern provinces in 1954 and systematically moved into the Plain of Jars. Because the tiny Royal Laotian Air Force (RLAF) had no aerial reconnaissance capability, the government sought help from the United States. Not yet directly involved, the United States did not dare use military reconnaissance aircraft, even though it recognized the urgent need for intelligence. The U.S. Air Attaché in Saigon was also accredited to Vientiane, traveling between the two capitals frequently. Because his VC-47 transport aircraft had a K-17C aerial camera in a vertical mount and a hand-held K-20 camera for oblique photographs, he became the U.S. reconnaissance force in SEA. Deviating slightly from his normal course, he photographed road junctions, fords, airstrips, and other objectives requested by the Royal Laotian Government. The older aircraft and camera combination produced good photography that provided considerable intelligence concerning the hostile forces.[2]

During January and February 1961, the Royal Thai Air Force (RTAF) flew six reconnaissance sorties over Laos with RT-33 aircraft. Because of their higher speed and better maneuverability, the jet aircraft had a greater probability of survival in the small arms environment of the Pathet Lao regions of Laos and their improved camera configuration produced far better photography than that of the old VC-47 transport. A modification of the Lockheed T-33 jet trainer, the RT-33 had a camera nose similar to that of the Korea-era RF-80, but a wire recorder and other electronic equipment replaced the trainer's rear seat. Furnished to many nations under the MAP, the RT-33 had a 1,500-mile range and good speed. It was an ideal aircraft for "limited war conditions." The United States decided to use U.S. Air Force crews to carry out the reconnaissance missions.[3]

In early April, the State Department notified Ambassador Winthrop G. Brown in Vientiane that the Air Force was moving an RT-33 to a Thai airfield to fly reconnaissance sorties over Laos and other portions of SEA as needed. Nicknamed Project Field Goal, the RT-33 and support personnel arrived at Udorn Royal Air Force Base (RTAFB) on 17 April 1961 to fly aerial reconnaissance missions to support the requirements of the U.S. attaches and friendly governments. PACAF chose barren Udorn RTAFB because it was the Thai base closest to Laos. The 15th Tactical Reconnaissance Squadron at Kadena Air Base, Okinawa, and the 45th Tactical Reconnaissance Squadron at Misawa Air Base Japan provided experienced reconnaissance pilots for 45-day periods to fly the RT-33 missions. The first Field Goal sortie on 24 April 1961 was highly successful, and the detachment completed 16 sorties before the ICC stopped the flights on 10 May.[4]

Because Nationalist China had been flying RF-101A aircraft over Communist China since 1957, the Voodoo was no stranger to the region. Four TAC RF-101Cs, part of an exercise in the Philippines, deployed to Don Muang on 6 June 1960 to photograph 10 objectives in Thailand for the Royal Thai Government.[5] Three RF-101Cs from Kadena Air Ease were flown to Takhli RTAFB on I March 1961 to participate in the Southeast Asia Treaty 0rganization (SEATO) Exercise Air Bull, but remained aloof from the Laos situation. After participating in an air show at Tan Son Nhut Air Base, they returned to Kadena Air Base on 9 March.[6] The Air Force had not committed the Voodoo to combat.

Pipe Stem

A request from the Government of South Vietnam for U.S. Air Force participation in an air show at Tan Son Nhut Air Base in 0ctober 1961 provided an opportunity to move RF-l0lCs into SEA legally. Sent from Kadena Air Base on short notice, four RF-10lCs from the 15th Tactical Reconnaissance Squadron landed at Tan Son Nhut Air Base on 18 0ctober, only to learn that the South Vietnamese Government had cancelled the air show. Support aircraft already had brought in maintenance and support personnel, tools, supplies, and a photo processing cell (PPC); the Vietnamese Air Force (VNAF) had allocated ramp space, billeting, and support facilities. The Pipe Stem Task Force, as the detachment had been nicknamed, was ready to fly.[7]

On one of its frequent rampages, the Mekong River overflowed its banks and flooded most of the delta in South Vietnam, causing widespread damage and extensive human suffering. At the request of the Government of South Vietnam, the Commander in Chief, Pacific Command (CINCPAC) told the Pipe Stem Task Force to stay at Tan Son Nhut Air Base for 8 days to photograph the flooded areas. At the same time, the Joint Chiefs of Staff (JCS) told the task force to photograph certain objectives in Laos – including the Plain of Jars and the Ho Chi Minh Trail – to satisfy the intelligence needs of a variety of U.S., Laotian, and South Vietnamese political and military agencies. The first sortie on 21 0ctober brought the RF-101Cs into the SEA war.[8]

Pipe Stem aircraft and personnel belonged to Fifth Air Force, but while in SEA they came under the operational control of Thirteenth Air Force from its headquarters at Clark Air Base in the Philippines. Major General Theodore R. Milton, Thirteenth Air Force commander, directed the Pipe Stem Task Force to photograph Tchepone Airfield on 23 October, apparently to confirm intelligence gathered from other sources. The RF-101Cs flew four sorties over Tchepone that day, bringing back photographic proof that Soviet IL-.|4 transport aircraft were parachuting supplies to the Pathet Lao and North Vietnamese. Two RF-101Cs on 25 October again photographed a single IL-14 over Tchepone, but encountered fairly accurate antiaircraft fire. Once more the photography showed the position of the drop; parachutes on the ground and in the air, aircraft identification markings, and the heading taken by the departing aircraft. When he saw the photographs, President John F. Kennedy ordered the reconnaissance sorties continued. [9]

Although prepared only for a short stay, the pipe Stem Task Force received some supplies and equipment and a few additional personnel from Okinawa and the Philippines. Fuel was particularly scarce, and even careful rationing could not prevent occasional grounding of one or more aircraft. Fortunately, the weather remained excellent over South Vietnam and generally good over Laos, enabling the task force to achieve a high percentage of success. Because Tchepone was only 30 minutes from Tan Son Nhut Air Base, and the farthest objective in the Plain of Jars about an hour away, most sorties were quite short. The pilots normally planned the missions at medium altitude, but the height of the cloudbases in the objective area determined the actual mission altitude. Aside from an occasional burst of antiaircraft fire, the sorties proved quite routine and the task force averaged more than two sorties per day, mostly over Laos.

Fully aware that the Government of South Vietnam had cancelled the air show and able to see that the Mekong River flood was subsiding, the ICC could not continue to ignore the RF-l01C activity. When it finally pressed for the withdrawal of the aircraft, the four RF-101Cs flew back to Kadena Air Base on 21 November, leaving the PPC behind. The Pipe Stem pilots had flown 67 successful reconnaissance missions in 31 days, photographing more than 75 percent of the assigned Laotian and South Vietnamese objectives. [10]

Able Mable

Although the Pipe Stem Task Force had been an expedient, it had proven the worth of modern jet reconnaissance aircraft in a counterinsurgency (COIN) situation and had emphasized the need for a more permanent capability in SEA. A study group headed by Presidential adviser General Maxwell Taylor in October 1961 had urged prompt support for the South Vietnamese Government, including the use of U.S. reconnaissance aircraft to collect intelligence. Expecting the ICC to oppose any renewed U.S. reconnaissance from South Vietnam at that time, the United States made other arrangements.

As early as 9 April 1961, the Royal Thai Government had agreed to a U.S. proposal to station three RF-101Cs at Takhli RTAFB to fly the reconnaissance sorties over Laos but the United States had taken no further action. Because the

ICC had halted the Field Goal RT-33 sorties over Laos, the Field Goal Task Force in July 1961 moved from Udorn RTAFB to Don Muang Airport for better aircraft maintenance facilities and housing. Continued pressure from the JCS finally resulted in a renewal of the daily overflight of Laos. A Field Goal RT-33 flew a sortie over the Plain of Jars on 4 October 1961. All factors considered, Thailand appeared to be the best potential base for a permanent U.S. reconnaissance effort over SEA at that time.

General Maxwell Taylor (left)consulting with President John F, Kennedy (right)
Courtesy of: John F Kennedy Memorial Library

General Theodore Ross Milton (December 29, 1915 - August 24, 2010) earned his pilot wings in March 1941. From 1943 to the end of hostilities in Europe, he served in B-17 aircraft with the Eighth Air Force in England. In 1961 he was promoted to major general and reassigned to Clark Air Base in the Philippines as commander, 13th Air Force, the parent command to all United States air bases in Southeast Asia. General Milton commanded Thirteenth Air Force until 1963. General Milton retired from the Air Force on July 31, 1974.

Source: U.S. Air Force.

General Paul Donal Harkins (May 15, 1904 - August 21, 1984) was Deputy Chief of Staff during World War II to George S. Patton Jr. and later became a U.S. Army general and the first Military Assistance Command, Vietnam (MACV) commander, serving in that role from 1962 to 1964. Harkins retired in 1964, and four years later worked for Twentieth Century Fox as a military advisor for the movie Patton. He became an accomplished painter and authored When the Third Cracked Europe, about the Third Army's route during World War II.

Source: U.S. Army

Brigadier General Stephen D. McElroy (October 2, 1912 - May 15, 1991) flew combat missions from Clark Field and the Florida Blanca Base in the Philippines as part of B-32 combat suitability tests. Postwar, he commanded the 376th Bombardment Wing (B-47) at Barksdale Air Force Base, La., for two years. On December 29, 1961, General McElroy was assigned as vice commander, 13th Air Force, at Clark Air Base in the Philippines. On May 15, 1962, he was assigned additional duties as commander, Air Force Component, Joint Task Force 116 and 6010th Tactical Group in Thailand. He retired in 1964.

Source: U.S. Air Force.

U.S. Ambassador Kenneth T. Young approach the Royal Thai Government in October 1961 with a proposal to station four RF-10lCs at Don Muang Airport for reconnaissance over Laos and South Vietnam. Having earlier proposed just such a move, the Thai Government gave immediate approval. The l5th Tactical Reconnaissance Squadron already was involved in Project Pipe Stem, so Fifth Air Force on 29 October told the 45th Tactical Reconnaissance Squadron to send four RF-101Cs to Don Muang Airport for 30 days as Task Force Able Mable. PACAF authorized a task force strength of 45 people, including seven RF-101C pilots and enough technicians to man a photo processing and interpretation facility (PPIF). Thirteenth Air Force already had established an advance echelon (ADVON) headquarters at Tan Son Nhut Air Base to control the growing number of Air Force units and people in SEA, and Detachment 10 of that ADVON managed U.S. Air Force activities at Don Muang Airport. The detachment provided the Able Mable Task Force with normal housekeeping support. The senior Able Mable pilot served as reconnaissance staff officer and RF-101 operations officer for Detachment 10, and was responsible for Able Mable Task Force missions.[II]

Four Able Mable RF-101Cs completed their move to Don Muang Airport on 7 November 1|961, having refueled at Kadena Air Base, Okinawa, and Clark Air Base, Philippines. An accompanying C-130 carried support personnel, supplies, and equipment. After the Field Goal RT-33 flew its final reconnaissance sorties that day, mechanics converted it to a courier aircraft for the delivery of photography and reports to Vientiane, Tan Son Nhut, and Clark Air Base under the nickname Mail Pouch. Able Mable RF-l0lC pilots flew their first Laos reconnaissance sortie on 8 November and soon achieved the specified three per day sortie rate. Although the pilots were experienced, they found their new sorties quite different from any they had flown previously, requiring very basic flying skills and considerable ingenuity.

Original members of the Able Mable Reconnaissance Task Force standing next to an RF-101C Voodoo at Don Muang RTAFB.

Source: U.S. Air Force

Don Muang Airport was both a major RTAFB and Thailand's largest commercial air terminal, used by 29 international air carriers in 1961. The commercial and military air traffic kept its single runway busy (although construction of a second parallel runway was nearing completion). Aircraft parking space was minimal, but other support facilities were excellent. A low-frequency radio beacon and runway lighting made all-weather operations possible. Bangkok was but a few miles away, connected by both road and railroad.

Of all the obstacles to reconnaissance over SEA, weather was the one the RF-l0lC pilots could do the least about. Royal Thai Navy weather specialists at Bangkok provided forecasts for Able Mable mission planning through an Air Force forecaster at Detachment 10. The forecasts for Thailand, most of the Laos panhandle, and southern North Vietnam were quite accurate, but there were no reporting stations in the northern mountains to furnish forecast data for those portions of northern Laos and North Vietnam where many reconnaissance objectives were located. Consequently, each month a number of reconnaissance pilots aborted their missions or achieved only partial success when they encountered unexpected poor weather.

Except for occasional small arms fire and two anti-aircraft concentrations, Laos was relatively safe for the RF-101Cs. The Plain of Jars and Tchepone Airfield had antiaircraft weapons effective to 5,000 feet, causing pilots on sorties to fly above that altitude. Some of the longer focal length cameras carried by the RF-l0lC made it possible to get good scale photography from altitudes above 15,000 feet, but the persistent cloud cover usually forced the use of other cameras at lower altitudes. A combination of the type of objective, the weather, the desired scale, and the type of cameras carried by each aircraft determined the mission altitude for the RF-l0lCs. [12]

Navigation over much of SEA was primarily dead reckoning updated by pilotage -- visual identification of prominent landmarks. Although modern electronic navigation aids simply did not exist, there were low-frequency radio beacons in Thailand at Bangkok and Ubon RTAFB, Laos at Vientiane, and South Vietnam at Qui Nhon, Saigon, and Danang. Inaccurate maps and charts often forced the pilots to conduct area searches to locate their objectives. The most reliable maps of South Vietnam and Laos for some time were those of the French Auto club; copies were carefully passed from pilot to pilot. Strict orders to avoid overflight of Burma, North Vietnam, Cambodia, and China aggravated an already delicate navigation problem. [13]

Although they daily flew over sparsely inhabited areas largely controlled by hostile forces or aborigines, the Able Mable pilots had no formal rescue or recovery support. A handful of Royal Laotian Air Force and civilian aircraft in Laos and a few U.S. Army helicopters in South Vietnam provided a limited rescue potential.

Even before the first RF-101C sortie over Laos, Ambassador Winthrop G. Brown in Vientiane on 6 November had prohibited reconnaissance flights over the plain of Jars without his permission. The first RF-l0lC missions, therefore, were directed toward the Ho Chi Minh trail, a maze of primitive roads, waterways, and foot paths through the mountains of eastern Laos. The Plain of Jars, however, contained the most significant military positions, and both CINCPAC and PACAF needed frequent reconnaissance to maintain a valid intelligence assessment. When he learned that the more modern RF-101Cs had replaced the RT-33, Ambassador Brown removed his restriction on reconnaissance over the Plain of Jars. [14]

Ambassador Brown continued to insist that reconnaissance aircraft over all of Laos stay at or above 40,000 feet to avoid detection, but that became academic when anti-aircraft weapons fired at an RF-101C at 40,000 feet over Vang Vieng. PACAF then proposed that all RF-101C sorties over Laos and South Vietnam remain at altitudes most consistent with flight safety and best mission results. Thirteenth Air Force headquarters personnel soon convinced the Ambassador that he should remove the 40,000-foot restriction and allow PACAF to select mission altitudes. [15]

Able Mable RF-101C pilots at first flew about 75 percent cent of their missions over Laos and 25 percent over South Vietnam, but those percentages soon reversed. The missions over South Vietnam involved crossing the Laos panhandle, photographing the assigned objectives, and returning to Don Muang Airport. Objectives in northern South Vietnam, however, stretched the fuel range of the RF-101Cs dangerously close to the limit and forced many of the pilots to land at Tan Son Nhut Air Base to refuel.

PACAF on 18 November had designated the Pipe Stem PPIF as 0perating Location Number Two (0L-2) for Able Mable. 0L-2 processed the film from RF-

101Cs landing at Tan Son Nhut Air Base for fuel and reloaded their cameras to enable them to fly another sortie while returning to Don Muang Airport. Pilots on missions to photograph high priority objectives in South Vietnam also landed at Tan Son Nhut Air Base to allow the OL-2 personnel to expedite film processing and exploitation. As the number of high priority reconnaissance requests increased, Able Mable in early December 1961, began keeping an RF-101C on strip alert at Don Muang Airport to provide more rapid response. The growing number of reconnaissance missions scheduled each day, plus the strip alert requirements, strained the task force's ability. There just were not enough RF-101Cs to satisfy all of PACAF's needs.[16]

Although the task force had flown for only 30 days, well before that time CINCPAC extended the project indefinitely. By the end of 1961, the task force pilots had flown more than 130 reconnaissance sorties over Laos and South Vietnam, exposing more than 53,000 feet of film. The 45th Tactical Reconnaissance Squadron, faced with an indefinite stay in SEA, decided to rotate its aircraft and pilots every 6 weeks to ease the aircraft maintenance workload and to share the experience among all the pilots. Each pilot averaged 15 to 20 sorties during his 6 weeks in Thailand, acquiring experience that he never could have gained from a normal training situation.[17]

Most of the RF-101Cs crossed into Laos at one of five border points, and each of those points led to specific objective areas. The Pathet Lao and North Vietnamese thus could predict with some certainty the objectives of each RF-101 even before the aircraft actually crossed the border. To make the Pathet Lao's defensive task even easier, 85 percent of the RF-101Cs were over their objectives during the same 2-hour period each day. That offered major advantages to the opponent. When PACAF headquarters learned of those standardized missions, it directed the mission planners to vary takeoff times, routes, altitudes, and similar operational factors on a random basis to confuse the Pathet Lao.[18]

Small arms fire hit four RF-101Cs within a few weeks, but none suffered serious damage. Ail were below 1,500 feet above ground level (AGL) over Laos when hit. Thirteenth Air Force headquarters reacted on 1 February 1962, directing that the Able Mable RF-101C pilots fly higher than 5,000 feet over roads and waterways to avoid further small arms fire damage. Three days later, however, Thirteenth Air Force headquarters abolished all altitude restrictions and again left mission tactics to the task force personnel.[19]

As another safety measure, Thirteenth Air Force headquarters ordered that teams of two RF-101Cs fly reconnaissance missions over Laos whenever possible, particularly those missions against transportation which seemed to produce the most ground fire. In addition to providing rescue control for the loss of one of the RF-101Cs, the two aircraft formation almost doubled the width of the swath photographed and greatly reduced the possibility of a camera system malfunction in one aircraft voiding the mission.[20]

Many standard concepts of tactical reconnaissance proved invalid. Conceived as pinpoint photography of carefully delineated objectives, prestrike reconnaissance more often than not required mosaic-type photography of a large area so the photo interpreters could search for elusive targets. Rather than dashing across a single spot, the RF-101C droned back and forth to expose hundreds of photographs, often while under sporadic small arms fire. Post-strike reconnaissance was equally frustrating because dense foliage soaked up bomb bursts, quickly hiding any damage. Reconnaissance in SEA was vastly different than it had been in the Korean conflict or much of World War II but the Able Mable team had to apply many old reconnaissance principles to new situations.[21]

One new requirement called for the RF-101C pilots to use a T-11 precision mapping camera to produce photography for the correction and construction of maps and charts. The T-11 camera could be fitted into the second camera bay in place of the three KA-2 cameras, but the RF-101C was not the stable camera platform needed for mapping. By March 1962, various agencies had asked Able Mable for more than 600 miles of T-11 mapping, but a controversy raged over whether the RF-101C pilots should do that type of photography. At Headquarters, 2d ADVON|, a provisional organization established at Tan Son Nhut Air Base to manage Air Force units in South Vietnam and Thailand, operations staff officers argued that photo mapping was a legitimate reconnaissance task as defined in AFM 55-6, and insisted that the RF-101Cs could accomplish the work more economically than special mapping aircraft. The Thirteenth Air Force headquarters staff and the intelligence staff officers at 2d ADVON headquarters argued that the intelligence requirements in SEA were far more important than mapping needs, and again pointed out the relative instability of the RF-101C as a mapping camera platform. For a time, at least, the intelligence advocates won and the T-11 camera was not installed or used.[22]

From time to time, practically every echelon proposed or made changes in the RF-101C camera system. For some missions, 24-inch or 36-inch focal length cameras replaced the oblique cameras of the fan array in the second camera bay. Air Force headquarters in early 1962 proposed mounting in some Able Mable RF-101Cs, KA-18 strip cameras in which the film moved constantly past a variable slit to produce a continuous photograph. The resultant photography was excellent for studying beach gradient, but entirely unsatisfactory for SEA intelligence needs. Faced with stiff opposition from 2d ADVON headquarters, Air Force headquarters withdrew the proposal.[23]

Meanwhile, PACAF decided that the 15th and 45th Tactical Reconnaissance Squadrons should share the Able Mable duty, changing responsibility every 6 months. As the first changeover neared, Thirteenth Air Force headquarters asked that the force be increased to six aircraft, but again PACAF simply did not have enough RF-101C's. As a consequence, the 15th Tactical Reconnaissance Squadron sent only four RF-101Cs from Kadena Air Base to Don Muang Airport on 23 May 1962 to relieve the 45th Tactical Reconnaissance squadron. [24]

Night Reconnaissance

Insurgent activities normally peaked either at night or under adverse weather conditions, both of which made aerial reconnaissance difficult or impossible. The

35

failure to equip the RF-101C for night photography became increasingly significant when General Paul D. Harkins, Commander, U.S. Military Assistance Command, Vietnam (COMUSMACV), asked that Able Mable fly night photographic missions. The Voodoo could do the job, but with some difficulty. Two 12-inch focal length KA-47 day/night cameras could replace the split vertical KA-1 cameras in the aft compartment. A C-1 photoelectric flash detector then replaced the B-2 terrain light detector, eliminating all automatic exposure settings for the other cameras. Finally, an external flash cartridge pod provided the necessary illumination.

Developed in 1954 for the Republic RF-84, the pod hung from an MB-7 external rack like an external fuel tank and could be jettisoned. Divided into two compartments, each of which held two racks, the pod carried a total of 80 M-123 photoflash cartridges. Openings in the bottom of the pod allowed the pilot to eject the cartridges. Though it was a makeshift combination on the RF-101C, it was the only night illumination capability the Voodoo could muster.[25]

At PACAF's request, Air Force headquarters in early 1962 authorized the modification of two RF-101Cs under Project Toy Tiger. The Toy Tiger conversion went beyond the mere installation of KA-47 night cameras and photoflash cartridge pods, replacing all cameras and modifying controls and mounts. A 6-inch focal length KA-45 camera replaced the KA-2 as a forward oblique camera in the nose compartment. A 3-inch KA-45 vertical camera and two 6-inch KA-45 oblique cameras replaced the three KA-2 cameras in the second compartment. The engineers also replaced the KA-1 split vertical camera in the aft bay with two 12-inch focal length KA-45 cameras with special high speed bodies. The Toy Tiger RF-101Cs also carried an RF-84 photo-flash cartridge pod externally. An APN-102/ASN-7 Doppler navigation computer, installed as part of the modification, slightly improved the navigation capability of the RF-101C.[27]

Although the modified aircraft reached Kadena Air Base in May 1962, PACAF postponed the tests when it learned that the 15th Tactical Reconnaissance Squadron had no film and no photo flash cartridges. By July, enough film was on hand to permit the squadron to carry out tests of the KA-45 day cameras over SEA. Because of depleted stocks, photoflash cartridges failed to arrive by 30 August; PACAF directed that subsequent test flights originate from Kadena Air Base. After the photoflash cartridges arrived in September, the 15th Tactical Reconnaissance Squadron again sent the Toy Tiger aircraft to Don Muang Airport for test missions over the Mekong River delta in South Vietnam.[23]

Almost immediately, the Army and Air Force photo interpreters protested the use of the M-45 cameras in the Toy Tiger aircraft. The new, smaller cameras produced negatives approximately 4-1/2 inches square, about one-fourth the area of the KA-2 camera negatives to which the photo interpreters and Army had become accustomed. The few night test missions had convinced 2d Air Division (the successor to 2d ADVON) that the photoflash cartridges produced too little light for successful night photography over SEA. Further, the great number of switches, dials, and indicators associated with the night camera equipment required the full attention of the pilot at a time when he should have been lining up for the run. Even before the tests were completed, however, the Cuban missile crisis caused Air Force headquarters to order the Toy Tiger RF-l0lCs to return to the United States for possible use over Cuba.[29]

Three days after the Pathet Lao on 9 May captured Nam Tha, Laos, CINCPAC activated JTF-116 under the contingency plan for the defense of Laos. With the Able Mable Task Force in place, there was no need to activate another reconnaissance task force. Thirteenth Air Force headquarters placed the RF-l0lCs under the operational control of Brigadier General Stephen D. McElroy, the JTF-116 Air Force component commander. Because it appeared likely that the Royal Laotian Government might at any time withdraw its permission for the Able Mable reconnaissance missions, the RF-101C pilots flew as many missions each day as weather and aircraft availability permitted. Considerable intelligence resulted from the missions. A mission on 27 July between Xieng Khouang and the North Vietnam border for example, photographed more than 300 trucks, 20 light tanks, and several Soviet cargo aircraft. Not every mission was quite so productive, but almost every mission produced some significant intelligence.[30]

Small arms fire continued to hit the RF-l0lCs but the damage usually consisted of one or two holes in some non-critical part. Good fortune ended on 14 August, however as an RF-l0lC flew a sortie along Route 7 at 8,000 to 10'000 feet AGL, apparently quite safe from the usual small arms fire. A 37mm or 57mm antiaircraft round suddenly slammed into the bottom of the fuselage and detonated under the pilot's seat, severing electric and hydraulic lines and damaging the right engine. The detonation also blew off the right camera access door which the Pathet Lao recovered and displayed as proof that the United States was violating Laotian territory. The uninjured pilot nursed the RF-l0lC back to Don Muang Airport, preferring to land where there was adequate crash equipment. His decision proved sound, because the nose gear collapsed on landing causing further damage. CINCPAC immediately halted all reconnaissance flights over Laos because of the danger to aircraft and pilots.[31]

CINCPAC waited two weeks before again authorizing limited RF-101C reconnaissance over Laos beginning on 1 September. The Able Mable RF-101Cs could not photograph objectives while en route to or from South Vietnam, and those objectives had to be south of 17° 30'N., which meant they could only be in the almost trackless southern half of the Laos panhandle. Further, the aircraft had to remain above 35,000 feet, and at that altitude even the longest focal length cameras produced negatives at a scale that made photo interpretation extremely difficult. About the only benefit accruing from the authorization was the ability to fly across Laos rather than detouring southward around Cambodia, saving several hundred miles of flying and time.[32]

Even that limited benefit was short-lived. While on a visit to SEA, General Maxwell Taylor, the Presidents military adviser, learned that if the North Vietnamese positioned a radar at or south of Vinh, they could track the Able Mable RF-l0lCs across Laos. There was no indication that such radars existed, but General Taylor was deeply concerned that the situation could embarrass the United States. On 14 September, therefore, he asked that all U.S. overflights of

Laos stop until the intelligence community could analyze the North Vietnamese radar "order of battle" and assure him that the RF-l0lCs crossing Laos would not be detected. Once more the Able Mable RF-101Cs flew south out of Bangkok on their long flight around Cambodia.[33]

Easing the restrictions only slightly, the JCS on 23 September 1962 again allowed the Able Mable RF-l0lC pilots to fly across Laos en route to South Vietnam, but required that they fly only from a point south of Pakse across the Mekong River to Bassac and south of Attopeu to the border, remaining above 35,000 feet. Six days later, CINCPAC lowered the minimum altitude to 20,000 feet, but ordered the RF-101C pilots to fly south of 15° N. Planners and pilots alike had a difficult time keeping abreast of the rapid changes dictated in Hawaii and Washington. The JCS on 6 November again terminated all U.S. reconnaissance overflight of Laos, once more forcing the RF-101C pilots to fly southward around Cambodia to reach South Vietnam. [34] The enemy, however, failed to take advantage of the situation and shifted his operations elsewhere.

Even though their infiltration routes through Laos were unobserved, the North Vietnamese sent increasing numbers of troops and ever larger quantities of supplies into and through the demilitarized zone (DMZ) separating North and South Vietnam. CINCPAC on 6 0ctober asked the JCS to approve the use of Able Mable RF-10lCs to photograph the demarcation line to verify the infiltration and supply stockpiling. CINCPAC wanted the Voodoos to make three runs--one at high altitude, one at about 9,000 feet, and a 'dicing' run at tree-top level. Approval finally came in early November with the provision that the aircraft were not to overfly Laos, either on the photo runs or en route to or from Thailand. Scheduled for the first good weather after l0 November, the mission required the RF-10lCs to fly south around Cambodia and stage from Tan Son Nhut Air Base.[35]

Both the JCS and the State Department had cited political reasons in rejecting several proposals to move the Able Mable Task Force to Tan Son Nhut Air Base. With overflight of Laos apparently ended, however, the move became highly desirable. 0n 15 November 1962, Thirteenth Air Force headquarters once more formally asked permission to move the Able Mable Task Force to Tan Son Nhut Air Base. The JCS already had authorized CINCPAC to station as many as four RF-101Cs at Tan Son Nhut Air Base, but asked that the aircraft be changed frequently in the hope that the ICC would not again press for removal of all U.S. aircraft. With JCS approval, CINCPAC ordered Able Mable to move to Tan Son Nhut Air Base not later than 15 December 1962. Minimal facilities for aircraft maintenance, camera repair, and photo processing would remain at Don Muang Airport to care for the RF-l0lCs that would occasionally land there. The Able Mable Task Force completed the move between 12 and 14 December without interrupting its flying schedule.[36]

Reconnaissance sorties from the new base were about half as long as they had been from Thailand, but aircraft use remained well above the desired maximum of 35 hours per aircraft per month. Since PACAF had only the two 16-aircraft squadrons of RF-101Cs, one-eighth of its force always was in SEA. Because deployments, exercises, and aircraft modification programs tied up another segment of the force, PACAF found it impossible to meet all of its reconnaissance obligations. Further, the four Able Mable RF-'101Cs consumed one-third of PACAF's monthly authorized RF-101C flying time, seriously limiting training and proficiency time for the remaining seven-eights of the force. PACAF asked Air Force headquarters to authorize 25 RF-l0lCs for each of the squadrons, but it allowed no changes at that time.[37]

Seeking to ease the situation, Thirteenth Air Force headquarters tried to replace the Able Mable RF-l0lCs. It asked that Air Force headquarters assign eight RF-84Fs with crews and support personnel to SEA. Four of the aircraft would replace the Able Mable RF-101Cs, while the remaining four would be based at Clark Air Base as a reserve aircraft pool. The RF-84F had acceptable range and an excellent camera system, and had been designed to operate from unimproved bases. Thirteenth Air Force headquarters was unable to sell its plan, however, and dropped the proposal.[33]

Even the type of missions adversely affected the number of requirements that the RF-l0lCs could satisfy. Most reconnaissance requests called for low-altitude photography of large areas, several kilometers on each side. The RF-101C pilots found themselves making back-and-forth runs over forested areas in which some intelligence officer hoped the enemy might be hiding, covering only one or two objectives on each mission and overloading the processing and interpretation facilities with hundreds of photographs per sortie. In early January 1963, 2d Air Division asked for two additional RF-101Cs to help with the growing request backlog. Both PACAF and CINCPAC approved the addition, but the JCS and the Secretary of Defense disapproved. The Able Mable Task Force continued to struggle along with four RF-l0lCs.[39]

Efforts to acquire additional RF-101Cs from other commands proved equally unsuccessful. Air Force headquarters in January 1963 proposed that United States Air Forces in Europe (USAFE) transfer two RF-l0lCs to the Able Mable Task Force and that TAC send one. USAFE proved amenable to the proposal, but TAC protested so strongly that Air Force headquarters dropped the idea. The JCS on 12 February told Strike Command to send three TAC RF-101Cs to the Able Mable Task Force but again TAC successfully opposed the move. The JCS withdrew their order when TAC showed that after deducting aircraft engaged in combat crew training, modification, and special maintenance, it had only 26 RF-l0lCs to meet its worldwide commitments. The Able Mable Task Force finally received augmentation in March when CINCPAC told PACAF to provide two additional RF-l0lC's. The 45th Tactical Reconnaissance Squadron moved two RF-l0lCs to Tan Son Nhut Air Base on 1 April 1963 to bring the task force up to its newly authorized strength of six.[40]

Even with the additional aircraft, the task force had more requests for aerial reconnaissance than it could handle. Strangely, although there were 10 times as many Army advisers in SEA in early 1963 as there had been a year earlier, they appeared reluctant to ask for Air Force aerial photography for planning purposes, particularly prior to operations involving Army helicopters, apparently feeling that the very presence of the RF-101Cs somehow would betray the pending operation.

Staff officers at 2d Air Division headquarters found themselves trying to sell RF-101C sorties to the Army in spite of the already overworked Voodoo aircraft and pilots.[41]

PACAF on 8 July 1963 assigned the Able Mable Task Force to the 33d Tactical Group at Tan Son Nhut Air Base, ending the long existence of the task force as a semi-autonomous operating body. The 33d Tactical Group in turn activated Detachment I to control all assigned reconnaissance aircraft, including the six Able Mable RF-l0lC's. The 2d Air Division reconnaissance staff officer commanded Detachment 1, and the senior RF-101C pilot served as operations officer. The two Fifth Air Force squadrons continued to furnish personnel and aircraft on temporary duty. Even though the Able Mable Task Force formally ceased to exist, the name persisted for the RF-l0lC contingent.[42]

Meanwhile, when the Able Mable Task Force sent two RF-101Cs to Don Muang Airport in late May 1963 to photograph several areas for the Royal Thai Government, it had to send along photo technicians and interpreters because the local PPC could not provide the required support. Conditions had improved somewhat by December 1963 when 2d Air Division again sent two RF-101Cs to Don Muang Airport for 7 days to photograph in Thailand. This time the local PPC processed most of the aerial film and shipped the remainder to Tan Son Nhut Air Base.[43]

Six RF-101Cs with crews and support personnel from the 45th Tactical Reconnaissance Squadron flew to Tan Son Nhut Air Base on 1 November 1963 to assume Able Mable duty, replacing the l5th Tactical Reconnaissance Squadron aircraft and personnel. The daily sortie rate was then about four or five per day, with one aircraft and pilot on alert during daylight hours. Although most missions were planned to satisfy existing requirements, scrambles by the alert RF-l0lCs became more numerous.[44]

Because the enemy owned the night, CINCPAC at the end of August 1963 proposed increased night reconnaissance over known enemy concentrations in Laos and South Vietnam, particularly the Viet Cong base areas northeast of Saigon. Unfortunately, the Air Force had no reliable night photographic capability. Early tests had affirmed that the jungles soaked up too much of the light from the photoflash cartridges, and the rice paddies reflected too much of the light. Although improvement was slow and gradual, by year's end the RF-l0lCs were taking acceptable night photographs of such prominent features as hamlets or outposts under attack and coastal shipping.[45]

At least a part of that coastal shipping ended up in Cambodia, a significant refuge and staging area for North Vietnamese and Viet Cong forces. The Cambodian leader, prince Norodom Sihanouk, professed total neutrality and the United States carefully avoided any violation of the Cambodian border. The commander of 2d Air Division in December 1963 told Secretary of Defense Robert s. McNamara that he had chosen 17 key areas along the border and planned to schedule RF-l0lCs to photograph them as frequently as possible to develop infiltration intelligence.

From flight paths over South Vietnam, the RF-l0lC pilots used long focal length oblique cameras to photograph objectives located some distance inside Cambodia. By the end of 1963, the Voodoos had photographed about 85 percent of the border with vertical and oblique cameras without violating Cambodian territory, which remained off limits to U.S. reconnaissance aircraft.[46]

Laos also remained closed to U.S. tactical reconnaissance aircraft and there appeared little hope that this restriction would be relaxed. The JCS on 22 January 1964 urged the Secretary of Defense to insist upon renewed reconnaissance overflight of Laos and a new program of overflight of Cambodia to secure intelligence essential to the defense of South Vietnam.[47] Ambassador Leonard Unger in Vientiane voiced his support for renewed reconnaissance over Laos as did the JCS on 27 February. The State Department, however, remained adamantly opposed. [48]

As the time arrived to swap Able Mable responsibility once more, it was handled differently. Four RF-l0lCs of the 15th Tactical Reconnaissance Squadron were sent to Don Muang Airport on 20 April 1964 as Reconnaissance Task Force (RTF) Bravo to take part in the Southeast Asia Treaty 0rganization (SEAT0) Exercise Air Boon Choo. The RTF pilots flew an average of six sorties per day over the next 6 days, achieving a 99 percent success rate. 0n 30 April, the RTF moved to Tan Son Nhut Air Base where it was joined by two more RF-l0lCs to form the new Able Mable Task Force.[49]

Yankee Team

Pathet Lao forces on 17 May 1964 suddenly attacked the Laotian Neutralist forces in the Plain of Jars and sent them reeling southward toward territory held by the Royal forces. By sunset the insurgents held most of the Plain of Jars, and the Laotian government faced a crisis. The United States casting about for some way to demonstrate its support for the legal government, proposed that U.S. reconnaissance aircraft fly sorties over the plain of Jars and other Pathet Lao areas. De-spite his fears that such a move might compromise his impartial leadership image, premier Souvannaphouma finally consented.[50]

Anticipating renewed reconnaissance missions over Laos, the JCS on 17 May 1964 had told CINCPAC to alert the RF-l0lC pilots at Tan Son Nhut Air Base and U.s. Navy carrier-based reconnaissance aircrews. The following day, the JCS told the Air Force to use RF-l0lCs on 19 May to photograph infiltration routes from North Vietnam through Laos into South Vietnam, placing particular emphasis on the Ban Thay military installation east of Muong Phine and contiguous roads and trails. The JCS set no limit on the number of sorties, but they did direct that air aircraft avoid overflight of North Vietnam even though objectives such as the Mu Gia pass were located close to poorly defined borders.[51]

Early on the morning of 19 May 1964, four RF-l0lC pilots took off from Tan Son Nhut Air Base and headed northward. Within a few minutes, the four Voodoos streaked low across the unmarked border and took the first photographs of the Laotian panhandle since December 1962. Maintaining a low altitude provided the best possible scale for the photo interpreters, the pilots quickly covered their assigned objectives and headed back toward Tan Son Nhut Air Base where technicians stood ready to process and exploit the film. The term "exploit" here includes the plotting and interpretation of aerial photography to derive as much as possible of the intelligence contained therein and includes enlarging the prints, preparing duplicates or transparencies, and such other manipulation as might be necessary to assist in the interpretation. Because of a dearth of major roads and other cultural features in the southern panhandle, the first missions produced no significant intelligence, but they demonstrated U.S. support for the legal government.[52]

Two days later, Navy RF8 aircraft from the carrier Kitty Hawk joined the Air Force RF-10lCs on reconnaissance sorties over the Plain of Jars and the roads connecting it with North Vietnam. The JCS specified the type and number of aircraft each service would use and the cameras each would carry leaving the local commanders little mission planning flexibility. The State Department announced that the Royal Laotian Government had asked for the sorties so it could give the ICC proof of the Pathet Lao violations of the Geneva agreements. The Air Force rushed photographs and reports to Vientiane and turned them over to the Royal Laotian Government.[53]

Headquarters of the Military Assistance Command, Vietnam (MACV) seized the opportunity to propose a continuing program of two daylight, low-altitude reconnaissance missions and one night mission each week over Laos. Although the Able Mable Voodoos could sustain some increased number of sorties for a few days, any permanent program such as MCV envisioned would require three additional RF-10lC aircraft. Ambassador Unger in Vientiane persuaded Premier Souvanna Phouma to approve continued reconnaissance missions over Laos, although Souvanna insisted that if the sorties caused unfavorable reactions, the United States would have to accept full responsibility for violating Laotian Sovereignty.[54]

Anticipating continuation of the Laos reconnaissance missions, the JCS on 22 May assigned the nickname Yankee Team to the program they were developing and established the criteria and restrictions that would govern the missions. When they approved the program on 25 May, the JCS stated four objectives. First, of course, the missions were intended to acquire timely, tactical intelligence for friendly forces in Laos. Second, as announced by the State Department, they were to substantiate, if possible, the extent and scope of North Vietnam's infiltration of war materiel and troops through Laos to South Vietnam. Next, the presence of U.S. reconnaissance aircraft over Laos would provide a psychological boost to friendly forces. Finally, the missions would demonstrate U.S. interest and determination to stay in SEA as long as the North Vietnamese aggression threatened the peace. The JCS also required that at least 36 hours prior to takeoff time each reconnaissance unit would advise them of the specific objectives the mission would cover, the rationale for those objectives, and a specific justification if the sortie rate exceeded nine during any 24-hour period.[55]

Neither the Air Force nor the Navy flew missions over Laos on 23 May, but CINCPAC scheduled individual -- six Air Force and three Navy--low-altitude reconnaissance sorties on 24 May to complete the coverage of key roads and infiltration routes, update information on the tactical situation, and fill the gaps in earlier coverage. Sorties continued on a daily basis as the reconnaissance force tried to catch up with the demand.[56]

As the objectives assigned to each mission increased, some pilots found it necessary to land at Da Nang Air Base for fuel. Because of crowded conditions and heavy air traffic at that base, such refueling stops frequently took more than two hours and caused an unacceptable delay in the receipt of photographs. For a time, an RF-101C or RB-57 waited at Da Nang Air Base for the reconnaissance aircraft and immediately flew the film to Tan Son Nhut Air Base for processing and exploitation. This proved wasteful of resources and time, so a better solution was worked out with the Navy. On 29 May, a Navy A3B aircraft refueled an RF-101C returning from a Yankee Team mission, speeding up mission completion. The Navy continued the airborne refueling missions until 9 June, when Air Force KC-97s took over the task.[57]

Aware that the Yankee Team program had greatly increased the workload of the six RF-101Cs in the Able Mable force, PACAF in May 1964 increased the force strength to 10 aircraft to make certain that it could keep 6 operational. The 15th Tactical Reconnaissance Squadron, having assumed Able Mable responsibility on 1 May, provided the additional aircraft. Also, three RF-101Cs modified by TAC to carry M-45 cameras in place of the KA-2 cameras for low-altitude, high-speed missions replaced three of the standard configuration RF-101Cs at Tan Son Nhut Air Base. The small format (4.5 by 4.5 inches compared to 9 by 18 inches of the KA-2) photographs continued to be unpopular with the photo interpreters, but the KA-45 cameras were used extensively for day missions.[58] Early in June 1964, Thirteenth Air Force told PACAF that if the demand for reconnaissance continued to grow, the Able Mable force would need further augmentation to keep 10 aircraft operational.

Navy reconnaissance aircraft met some of the demands, but encountered difficulty. Hostile antiaircraft fire downed a Navy RF-8E in the Plain of Jars on 6 June 1964, causing the JCS to order fighter escort for later reconnaissance missions. Anti-aircraft fire also downed a Navy F-8 escort aircraft the next day, causing a temporary halt to all Laotian missions. The JCS on 9 June told CINCPAC to launch a strike force of eight F-100Cs to attack the antiaircraft positions at Xieng Khouang as a warning to the North Vietnamese and Pathet Lao. An RF-101C photographed the strike, and the 2d Air Division rushed the prints and reports to Washington. At Premier Souvanna Phouma's request, Ambassador Unger cancelled all missions scheduled for 10 June and subsequent days.[59]

Quickly changing his mind, Souvanna Phouma on 11 June .1964 told Ambassador Unger that he wanted the United States to resume reconnaissance missions over Laos on the following day without fanfare or publicity. It was 14 June, however before an RF-101C, escorted by four F-100s, again flew a reconnaissance mission over portions of the Laotian panhandle and the Plain of Jars. After a stand-down of almost 2 weeks, on 27 June two RF-101Cs one modified to carry the KA-45 cameras, flew over Laos with an escort of four armed F-100s. Immediately

43

thereafter, CINCPAC announced that the two missions had so updated his intelligence files that he would need only an occasional mission to keep them current.[60] That pronouncement, coupled with the earlier loss of two Navy aircraft, caused the JCS to stop all aerial reconnaissance over Laos. On the 9 days in June on which they had flown reconnaissance missions over Laos, the RF-101Cs had completed 35 sorties, many of which photographed large truck convoys entering Laos from North Vietnam.[61]

Regular Yankee Team reconnaissance missions resumed in early July, but the pilots found the antiaircraft threat significantly increased. Photography of Ben Thuot on 11 July showed six new 57mm antiaircraft guns in position, and photography of Ban Ban a week later revealed six more 57mm guns and a possible Firecan fire-control radar Photography also disclosed additional 37mm guns at Khang Khay on 20 July, increasing the low altitude threat. Antiaircraft fire damaged an RF-101C in a low altitude reconnaissance mission over Nhommarath on 31 July, but the escorts attacked the position and silenced the guns.[62]

North Vietnamese 57mm anti-aircraft site at Ban Ban.

Source: U.S. Air Force

Headquarters 2d Air Division on 1 August began scheduling a daily RF-101C weather reconnaissance mission over all portions of Laos at high altitude to determine whether there was a reasonable chance of reconnaissance success. Although their RF-101Cs carried loaded cameras, the weather mission pilots were not allowed to photograph objectives or targets of opportunity. Reconnaissance missions waited on the ground until the weather scout reported weather in the objective areas good enough for photography. Some PACAF headquarters staff officers complained that the weather reconnaissance sorties used too many RF-101C flying hours, but others contended that they saved many sorties that otherwise might have been wasted. CINCPAC asked why F-100, F-105, or RF-57 aircraft and crews could not fly the weather reconnaissance sorties just as well as the RF-101C pilots, but the reconnaissance staff contended that only a trained reconnaissance pilot could evaluate such factors as haze, light intensity, and cloudcover.[63]

While the Yankee Team program had evolved in Laos, aerial reconnaissance in Vietnam gradually had expanded and some bad habits had crept into the system. Reconnaissance training for RF-101C pilots had emphasized taking the fewest possible photographs to cover each objective, but in SEA they had begun turning on their cameras long before reaching each objective and letting them run well past it. Although they increased their chances of success, they also greatly increased the amount of film to be processed and exploited. PACAF head-quarters later began to measure the success of a mission by the amount of film exposed rather than the number of objectives successfully photographed.[64]

PACAF in August increased the Able Mable strength to 12 RF-101Cs to counter the growing number of reconnaissance requests and the fewer objectives being covered by each sortie. As a result, the 15th Tactical Reconnaissance Squadron had most of its RF-101Cs and personnel on temporary duty in SEA. When North Vietnamese torpedo boats attacked U.S. Navy destroyers in the Gulf of Tonkin on 2 and 4 August 1964, PACAF immediately ordered four additional RF-101Cs from Kadena Air Base and two from Misawa Air Base to augment the Able Mable force. To partially rebuild the reconnaissance force at Kadena Air Base, TAC sent six RF-101Cs of the 20th Tactical Reconnaissance Squadron to Okinawa. Two replacement RF-101Cs for the 15th Tactical Reconnaissance Squadron also took part in the flight across the Pacific. When the detachment arrived on 9 August, the 313th Air Division commander immediately alerted them for possible duty at Tan Son Nhut Air Base should the situation deteriorate further.[65]

In at least one aspect, the situation already had worsened. When a U-2 pilot on 7 August photographed Phuc Yen Airfield, North Vietnam's principal military air base, the film revealed a number of MiG-15 and MiG-17 fighter aircraft, a significant new threat to the unarmed RF-101Cs.[66] The immediate result was a change in the ordnance of the Yankee Team F-]00 escort aircraft to a mixture suitable for both air-to-air and air-to-ground combat operations. CINCPAC authorized U.S. forces to attack and destroy any hostile aircraft that attacked or threatened U.S. forces, and to conduct hot pursuit of hostile aircraft within certain limits.[67]

Missions into northern Laos stretched the range limits of the RF-l0lCs and increased the need for aerial refueling, making launch bases in Thailand and northern South Vietnam more appealing. In addition, 2d Air Division wanted to be able to launch RF-101Cs from more than one base to vary the pattern into which those sorties had settled by mid-l964. On 22 September, 2d Air Division headquarters proposed moving six RF-l0lCs to either Don Muang Airport or Udorn RTAFB, using fighter escort aircraft from either Takhli or Korat RTAFB and tanker aircraft from Takhli RTAFB. Such a move would provide greater flexibility in mission planning, shorter missions, and reduced refueling requirements.[68] Unfortunately, Ambassador Unger and the State Department opposed any extension of the reconnaissance program over Laos at that time. On 28 0ctober, however, Ambassador Unger reluctantly agreed that RF-101s and other Yankee Team reconnaissance aircraft could fly sorties over northern Laos, an area then designated Barrel Roll.[69]

Meanwhile, despite the unpopularity of the Toy Tiger RF-l0lC modification, Air Force headquarters directed that all RF-l0lCs be modified under Project ll81 – a modification that varied only slightly from Toy Tiger. Project ll81 retained the M-1 split vertical cameras, but replaced all other cameras with the small format KS-72s and a panoramic KA-56A camera. Slow delivery of cameras and accessories by the manufacturer delayed modification of the 45th Tactical Reconnaissance Squadron aircraft, the first to be converted in PACAF, making the squadron unable to take over Able Mable duties on I November 1964 as planned. PACAF delayed the changeover date until 1 February 1965, and left the 15th Tactical Reconnaissance Squadron in SEA. The latter thus became the first squadron to lose an RF-l0lC in combat.

On 21 November, Captain Burton Walz was over Ban Phan Nop photographing gun positions that had downed an F-100 3 days earlier when ground fire struck his RF-l0lC, causing it to burst into flames and begin tumbling out of control. Captain Walz ejected, but his parachute caught in one of the tall jungle trees, suspending him high above the ground. As he tried to secure himself, the canopy tore loose and he fell to the ground, breaking a leg and an arm and suffering other injuries. Fortunately, an Air America helicopter found him and flew him back to Korat RTAFB for medical treatment. 70

Two Royal Laotian Air Force T-28 aircraft disappeared on a strike mission on 19 November and an extensive search failed to find them. At Ambassador Unger's request, on 24 November two separate flights of two RF-l0lCs photographed the entire T-28 route from altitudes between 10,000 and 15,000 feet, with particular emphasis on the more mountainous regions of eastern Laos and western South Vietnam. When the photography failed to produce any evidence of the T-28s, 2d Air Division terminated the air search.[71]

As troops, equipment, and supplies continued to pour down the maze of narrow dirt roads and footpaths in eastern Laos that constituted the Ho Chi Minh Trail, RF-l0lCs photographed the infiltration at every opportunity. photography in late 1964 and early 1965 showed road improvement, bridge construction, and occasional dust clouds or glimpses of groups of people, all of which indicated growing use of the total trail system. Because the monsoon rains rendered the trail unusable for many weeks, the North Vietnamese moved every possible soldier and truckload of supplies while the dry weather persisted.

Mu Gia Pass, a vital section of the Ho Chi Minh infiltration route, was defended by antiaircraft guns and automatic weapons to ward off both reconnaissance and strike aircraft. On 17 January 1965, for example, an RF-101C and two F-105 escorts were over Mu Gia Pass when automatic weapons barrage fire began in their vicinity. The Voodoo pilot remained at 10,000 feet while the two F-105 pilots went in at 400 to 500 knots at tree-top level to strafe and bomb the offending gun positions. The tactic worked and was used frequently under similar circumstances as the reconnaissance missions continued to watch and measure the infiltration flow.[72]

Intelligence sources identified parts of three North Vietnamese Army (NVA) divisions in South Vietnam in early 1965, proof that men and supplies were moving southward over the trail. Most of the NVA and Viet Cong units in South Vietnam replaced their mélange of American, German, and homemade weapons with Communist bloc 7.62mm weapons, greatly increasing their firepower. At the same time, however, they became dependent upon a constant flow of ammunition down the trail from North Vietnam.[73]

Unfortunately, the RF-101Cs photographing the Ho Chi Minh Trail were normally restricted to medium altitudes, diminishing the effectiveness of their photography. Typical objectives, such as short log bridges or small piles of fuel drums, were usually well hidden beneath jungle canopy or camouflage, and could not be seen by the vertical cameras from 10,000 feet or above. Had the RF-101Cs been scheduled for "dicing" missions, the cameras could have looked under the concealing vegetation to record enemy positions. The JCS, however, considered low altitude missions too risky. As 1964 ended, the Voodoos remained active over South Vietnam and Laos, but political factors limited them to far less than their total capability.

CHAPTER III. RECONNAISSANCE OVER THE NORTH

Armed reconnaissance areas, referred to as Route Packages, were designed for the purpose of fixing responsibility for target development, collection of intelligence data, and target analysis in overall control of the Commander in Chief Pacific (CINCPAC). To ensure economical and effective use of resources, operational procedures have been developed by the operating units, 7th Air Force and Carrier Task Force 77, that permit the full range of coordination for all air operations in the Rolling Thunder program and yet permit both services to operate in all areas. Assigned areas of responsibility at that time [summer 1966] were U.S. Military Assistance Command Vietnam (COMUSMACV) for Route Package I, Pacific Fleet (PACFLT) for Route Packages II, III, IV and VIB, and Pacific Air Forces (PACAF) for Route Packages V and VIA. The two dark circles in Route Pack 6A and Route Pack 6B are "downtown" – the areas covered by the densest and most dangerous air defense system anywhere in the world at that time.
Source: U.S. Air Force Museum Web Collection

During late 1964 and early 1965, PACAF and Thirteenth Air Force became involved in an intensive and extended dialogue concerning a realignment of the RF-101C force in southeast Asia (SEA). Because the force at Tan Son Nhut Air Base was too large and too far from the objectives in northern Laos and North Vietnam, Thirteenth Air Force headquarters proposed transferring part of the force to either Don Muang Airport or Udorn RTAFB in Thailand. The Air Attaché in Bangkok protested the use of Don Muang Airport, however, citing its crowded aircraft parking space, lack of billeting, shortage of water, and the planned movement of KC-135,s to that base. The 18th Tactical Fighter Wing, parent unit of the 15th Tactical Reconnaissance Squadron, sent a team to Udorn RTAFB to determine if it was suitable for extended operations by RF-101Cs. The team found that the runway was too short and did not have an arresting barrier, and there was not enough water for the photo processing facilities or an adequate chemical waste disposal system. By the end of January 1965, though, PACAF had obtained authority for high priority construction at Udorn RTAFB and a realignment of the reconnaissance force.[1]

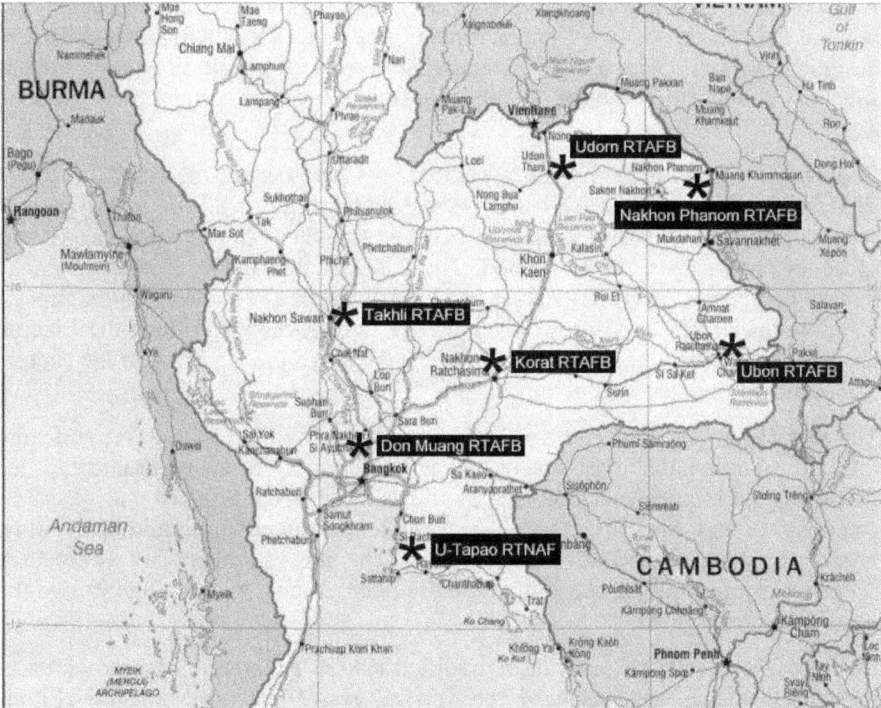

Royal Thai Air Force bases (RTAFB) and Royal Thai Naval Air Force (RTNAF)
bases used by the U.S. Air Force during the Vietnam War.
Source: U.S. Air Force.

Under the realignment, the 45th Tactical Reconnaissance Squadron on I February 1965 would move eight of its RF-101Cs to Tan Son Nhut Air Base and would maintain a capability to add four more Voodoos within 48 hours. This force was to be known as Able Mable Alpha. As soon as Udorn RTAFB became safe for RF-l0lC operations, the l5th Tactical Reconnaissance Squadron would send six RF-l0lCs that had been modified to carry the KA-45 cameras as Able Mable Bravo. Able Mable Alpha would concentrate on reconnaissance within South Vietnam and southern Laos, while Able Mable Bravo would fly Yankee Team missions over Laos and be able to extend into North Vietnam should such missions be authorized. The 2d Air Division commander would exercise operational control over both forces.2

Able Mable Alpha

Right on schedule, the 45th Tactical Reconnaissance Squadron sent eight RF-101Cs to Tan Son Nhut Air Base on 1 February 1965 to relieve the l5th Tactical Reconnaissance Squadron from Able Mable duty. These Voodoos had undergone the 1181 modification at a cost of $187,000 per aircraft for newer cameras and camera control systems. Some equipment problems remained unsolved when the modified RF-l0lCs reached SEA.

A Hycon KS-72 camera with a 6-inch focal length lens replaced the KA-2 forward oblique camera in the nose compartment. The new KS-72, a framing camera designed for both day and night photography, produced negatives only 4.5 inches square -- one-fourth of the area of the large format negatives produced by the KA-2.

Capable of taking as many as six photographs per second, the KS-72 had two shutters: for day photography, a focal plane shutter with speeds up to 1/4000 of a second; and for night photography, a between-the-lens shutter with a maximum speed of one-hundredth of a second. The KS-72A film magazine had an image motion compensation (IMC) feature and held as much as 500 feet of film, enough for more than 1,200 exposures. Two new KS-72 cameras with 6-inch focal length lenses also replaced the two KA-2 oblique cameras of the fan array in the camera compartment just forward of the cockpit.

The first Hycon KS-72A cameras had an unacceptably high failure rate and were difficult to maintain. The clutch brakes in the film drive mechanism failed frequently and excessive moisture in the camera body affected the electrical components and the film itself. The trouble continued until mid-year, when improved cameras (KS-72C1) were received. The new equipment had an excellent reliability record and produced high quality photography, even though it used the small format negatives.

Designed for the RF-4C aircraft, a modified KA-56 panoramic camera with a 3-inch focal length lens replaced the vertical KA-2. Intended for low-altitude photography, the KA-56A used a rotating prism ahead of the lens to produce a side-to-side photograph from horizon to horizon on a negative 41 inches by 9 inches. It could take as many as six photographs per second at shutter speeds up to 1/5,000 of a second. Fore and aft movement of the lens during exposure provided IMC, and the designers had added a potential for data annotation in-flight film processing, and film cassette ejection. The latter two characteristics, when perfected, would allow the pilot to automatically process the exposed film in the camera and drop the processed film to the ground commander who had asked for the reconnaissance, saving days of processing, exploitation, and delivery time. Use of such a film cassette would reduce the film capacity from the normal 1,000 feet to 250 feet. Tests showed the camera to be reliable and capable of good photography but the photo interpreters at first had some difficulty interpreting the distorted oblique images at both ends of each photograph.

Other cameras also were considered in various positions for possible future use. A Fairchild T-11 precision mapping camera with a 6-inch metrogon lens in an ART-21 torque-stabilized mount could replace the KA-56A, as could a 10-184 strip camera with either a stereo or unit lens arrangement. KS-72C cameras with 3-inch or 12-inch focal length lenses could replace the 6-inch KS-72's. The numerous possible camera combinations made the RF-101C a highly versatile vehicle capable of meeting almost any type of tactical reconnaissance requirement except night photography.[3]

Unpopular from the very first, the small format cameras increased processing workloads, complicated exploitation procedures, and intensified the tendency of the pilots to expose more film than necessary. The cameras were most effective below 8,000 feet or above 20,000 feet, leaving the optimum operating altitude of the RF-l01C without an effective camera. The photo interpreters continued to dislike the small negatives and the poor scale of the photography, and many Army officers who asked for Air Force reconnaissance specified that they would accept only the larger format photography.[4]

After the torpedo boat attacks on U.S. Navy destroyers in the Gulf of Tonkin in August 1964; the JCS drew up plans for retaliatory strikes should the North Vietnamese repeat such attacks or attack other U.S. installations or units. When the smoke cleared after a Viet Cong attack on the U.S. Army compound at Pleiku on 7 February 1965, eight U.S. personnel were dead and 109 wounded. The losses triggered the contingency plans and RF-l0lCs launched at once on weather reconnaissance missions. They found visibility at the targets in the panhandle of North Vietnam to be about a mile. The clouds began at 100 feet, and were solid up to 6,000 feet. Because bombing of small, vaguely defined targets under such conditions was out of the question, Lieutenant General Joseph H. Moore, 2d Air Division commander, delayed launching the strike force. An RF-101C on a reconnaissance mission and four RF-l0lCs intended as pathfinders launched from Tan Son Nhut Air Base on schedule, but General Moore had them recalled. When VNAF A-1 aircraft attacked the Chap Le Barracks early the next morning, however, an RF-101C went ahead of the force on a weather reconnaissance mission and two RF-l0lCs provided post-strike reconnaissance of the targets.[5]

Viet Cong explosives destroyed a U.S. billet at Qui Nhon on 10 February 1965, triggering another retaliatory strike against North Vietnam. When weather scout RF-l0lCs found good weather in the target area, the strike and support aircraft took off. The RF-l0lC reconnaissance aircraft photographed the target so soon after the bombing that the smoke and dust precluded bomb damage assessment (BDA). CINCPAC asked for authority to schedule another BDA reconnaissance mission but the JCS denied the request.[6]

Headquarters 2d Air Division on 18 February 1965 issued an operations order, nicknamed Racing Motor, to define reconnaissance participation in future retaliatory strikes against North Vietnam. The pilots of RF-101C weather reconnaissance aircraft were to pass target weather to the 2d Air Division Command Post at least an hour before the first scheduled strike aircraft take off. Escorted pathfinder RF-101Cs would precede the flak suppression aircraft to the target areas to acquire pre-strike photography, identify the target for the strike aircraft, and loiter in the area long enough to obtain immediate post-strike photography. Ignoring the lesson of the first BDA missions in North Vietnam, 2d Air Division again scheduled the post-strike reconnaissance too soon after the strike.[7]

Although 2d Air Division then cancelled Racing Motor before the squadrons could undertake it, CINCPAC issued new instructions that improved the situation BDA reconnaissance missions continued to accompany or follow closely behind the strike force, but CINCPAC authorized additional post-strike reconnaissance missions at the first good weather without the need for further approval. The RF-101Cs had to remain at medium altitude, and escort aircraft were not to be used. Two RF-101Cs photographed the USAF and VNAF strikes on the Quang Khe naval base on 2 March, but once again smoke and dust kept the photo interpreters from evaluating the damage.[8]

On 18 March 1965, the JCS authorized the Air Force and Navy to fly daily reconnaissance sorties over North Vietnam south of 20° N. Such flights, nicknamed Blue Tree, could carry out weather, visual, photographic, infrared, radar, and other sensor reconnaissance missions as appropriate, but had to fly above 10,000 feet AGL. CINCPAC protested the altitude restriction, pointing out that persistent heavy cloudcover and low ceilings would make medium altitude reconnaissance non-productive as much as 60 percent of the time. Subsequently the JCS on 30 March authorized low-altitude reconnaissance over North Vietnam and expanded to 21° N. where U.S. aircraft could fly reconnaissance missions, but prohibited all flights within 40 nautical miles of Haiphong or Phuc Yen Airfield. PACAF and 2d Air Division could provide fighter escort for the RF-101Cs but could schedule flak suppression aircraft only with JCS approval on an individual mission basis. The JCS also imposed a limit of 10 missions of two reconnaissance aircraft each per week.[9]

Able Mable Alpha RF-101Cs in April became the first Air Force tactical aircraft whose pilots used ECM against North Vietnam. When the JCS on 15 April authorized the use of active ECM against non-communications targets in North Vietnam, the Air Force quickly moved QRC-160 ECM pods and supporting personnel to Tan Son Nhut Air Base to support strike and reconnaissance operations. On 29 April, three RF-101Cs, each carrying four QRC-160 pods, supported a Rolling Thunder strike mission by jamming radars associated with defensive equipment. The new capability decreased the risk to strike aircraft, but it also further overworked the small force of RF-101Cs at Tan Son Nhut Air Base.[10]

(Note: Unfortunately, the original photographs used to illustrate this section have deteriorated so badly that they were completely illegible and Defense Lion

Publications was unable to find the originals. We have therefore inserted new pictures that show similar scenes.)

Bridges on the Ho Chi Minh Trail, note the bomb crates. The U.S. Air Force bombed key points on the Ho Chi Minh Trail. Source: U.S. Air Force

Bomb damage assessment photograph showing destroyed bridge and shallow crossing after being, bombed repeatedly.

Source: U.S. Air Force

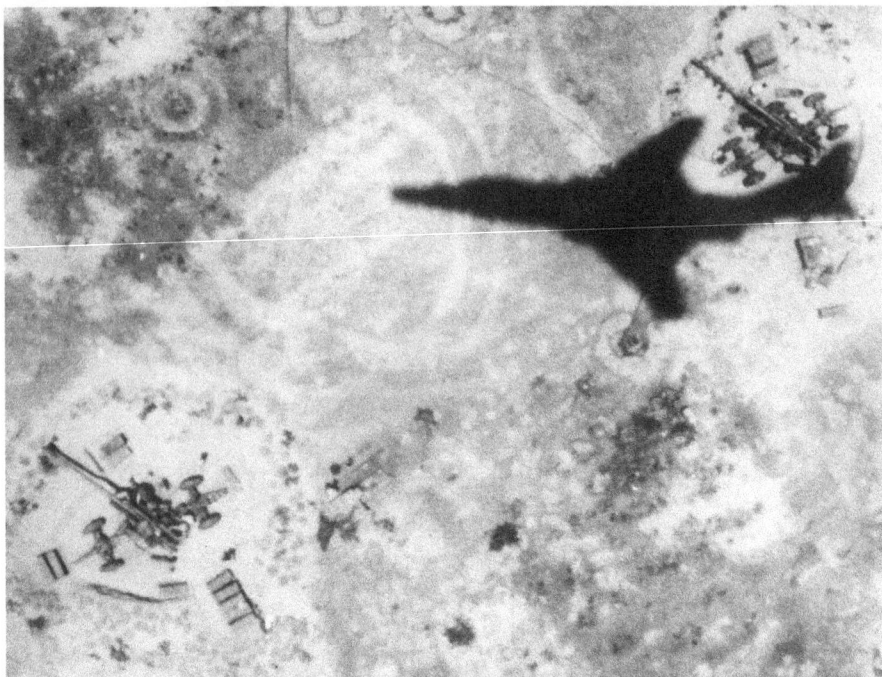

A part of the threat facing RF-101C pilots overflying North Vietnam. An anti-aircraft battery equipped with 57mm guns. Source U.S. Air Force.

A deadlier threat. A SA-2 Guideline anti-aircraft missile with its crew: Source U.S. Air Force.

Hanoi, July 1967. Source: Central Intelligence Agency

SA-2 Site Outside Hanoi: Source U.S. Air Force

Phuoc Yen Airfield just outside Hanoi. This Bomb Damage Assessment picture was taken too soon – the bombs are still going off.

Source: U.S. Air Force.

A better-timed picture shows what was left (not much) of the warehouses on the Haiphong waterfront after the F-105s had finished with them.
Source: U.S. Air Force

Green Python

Because of the events in North Vietnam, PACAF increased the Able Mable force at Tan Son Nhut Air Base to 12 RF-101Cs in late March. To avoid confusion, PACAF changed the nickname of the force at Udorn RTAFB to Green Python, while the force at Tan Son Nhut Air Base became just plain Able Mable once more. Four RF-101Cs from the 15th Tactical Reconnaissance Squadron arrived at Udorn RTAFB on 31 March, and two more arrived the next day to bring the force to full strength. With support personnel and equipment on hand, Green Python pilots flew their first Yankee Team reconnaissance mission from Udorn RTAFB on I April 1965.

Within a week, the force was fully operational and flying an average of four sorties per day. 0n 6 May, six 363d Tactical Reconnaissance RF-101Cs, then on temporary duty at Kadena Air Base, flew to Udorn RTAFB for a stay of 5 to 7 days. When the Royal Thai Government authorized an increase in the Green Python task force strength to 12 aircraft, the temporary duty of the 363d aircraft and crews became indefinite.[11]

At midnight on 12 May 1965, Saigon time, President Lyndon B. Johnson halted all bombing missions over North Vietnam, ostensibly to encourage Hanoi to enter into peace negotiations. The next day the Air Force and the Navy began an intensified reconnaissance campaign over North Vietnams flying |84 missions in 3 days. The large number of missions apparently caused the North Vietnamese to shift to night convoy operations, following a practice established in Laos. When the bombing resumed on 18 May, CINCPAC proposed continuing the intensive reconnaissance program over North Vietnam to ferret out hidden roads, trails, and other transportation and communication targets. [12]

April photography showed the first surface-to-air missile (SAM) sites under construction south of Hanoi. The Voodoo pilots had avoided small arms fire by flying above its effective range, and had largely overcome the antiaircraft fire by speed and course changes, but they could only guess at how effective the new missiles might be. 0n 5 May, a U-2 pilot photographed another almost completed SAM site 15 nautical miles southwest of Hanoi, and 10 days later the site was occupied. At lease three more missile sites had been completed by the end of May. The RF-101C pilots could not photograph the new missile sites because they were within the 40-nautical-mile circles around Haiphong and Phuc Yen Airfields, but their missions outside those circles occasionally took them within missile range. The danger area expanded on 24 July when a missile downed an F-4 several miles west of Hanoi. [13]

Even though the North Vietnamese Air Force had stationed MIG aircraft at Phuc Yen Airfield for several months, those aircraft never had presented more than a potential threat to the unarmed RF-101C's. CINCPAC, however, concerned that the fighter threat might suddenly increase without his knowledge, in 1965 directed daily photo coverage of all jet-capable airfields in North Vietnam above 20° N. to provide constant monitoring of the fighter aircraft inventory. An "odd-even" agreement between the Air Force and the Navy provided for full daily coverage of the airfields, with the Green Python RF-101C pilots responsible for photography on the odd days of the month. Photography from an 18 September mission showed eight MIG fighters at Kep Airfield, 35 nautical miles northeast of Hanoi, and 24 newly arrived aircraft shipping crates at Phuc Yen Airfield. The threat thus had increased considerably and would increase even more once the North Vietnamese assembled the new aircraft. [14]

Antiaircraft fire constituted the greatest threat, however, as the number of gun positions in North Vietnam grew at an alarming rate. The North Vietnamese made most effective use of their gun batteries by massing them around certain key target areas and along the routes used by strike and reconnaissance aircraft. They then began to use barrage fire coordinated with ground observer reports of low-flying U.S. aircraft, hoping that the aircraft would run into the massed projectiles. This tactic used enormous quantities of ammunition, but it was effective against the RF-101Cs as long as the pilots flew low-altitude sorties at or above 1,500 feet.[15]

Although interest centered on aerial reconnaissance over North Vietnam, the Green Python Task Force also continued to be responsible for most of Laos. Headquarters 2d Air Division directed that all reconnaissance missions above 18° N. be escorted by F-105 aircraft, which had a much shorter range than the RF-101C and could not loiter in the objective areas of northern Laos while the Voodoos took their pictures. The Green Python Task Force asked that 2d Air Division headquarters delete the escort requirement and allow the RF-101Cs to fly reconnaissance missions over northern Laos in pairs. As soon as 2d Air Division headquarters agreed, the two aircraft loose formation once more became standard over Laos.[16]

Growing Pains

RF-4C aircraft arrived at Tan Son Nhut Air Base in October 1965 to augment the RF-101C's, and the expanding reconnaissance force dictated a more permanent arrangement of the RF-101C units.

From October 1965, the RF-101C force was supplemented by RF-4C aircraft.
Source: U.S. Air Force

A complicated series of moves took place early in November. First, the 45th Tactical Reconnaissance Squadron, operating as Able Mable at Tan Son Nhut Air

Base, moved its aircraft and personnel back to Misawa Air Base, Japan. The 20th Tactical Reconnaissance Squadron, without aircraft, moved from Shaw Air Force Base to Tan Son Nhut Air Base, where it took over the Able Mable mission. The 15th Tactical Reconnaissance Squadron was to keep 12 operational RF-101C aircraft at Tan Son Nhut Air Base at all times for use by the 20th Tactical Reconnaissance Squadron, which, in turn, had to fly 14 sorties per day and keep an RF-101C and pilot on constant alert during daytime hours. In addition, the 15th Tactical Reconnaissance Squadron, with personnel assistance from the 45th Tactical Reconnaissance Squadron, had to man the Green Python Task Force at Udorn RTAFB on a temporary duty basis. The six RF-101Cs and crews from the 363d Tactical Reconnaissance Wing, then on temporary duty at Udorn RTAFB, returned to Kadena Air Base.[17]

The Voodoo missions were successful despite the complex mission planning and scheduling system under which they operated. The RF-101Cs at Udorn RTAFB and Tan Son Nhut Air Base were on loan from Fifth Air Force, and 2d Air Division actually owned only the one squadron of RF-4Cs that had arrived at the end of October 1965. Thirteenth Air Force headquarters earlier had proposed activating a reconnaissance wing at Tan Son Nhut Air Base to control all tactical reconnaissance assets in SEA, but PACAF wanted a reconnaissance wing at Tan Son Nhut and one at Udorn RTAFB. After considerable discussion, PACAF on 18 February 1966 activated the 460th Tactical Reconnaissance Wing at Tan Son Nhut Air Base, subordinating it to 2d Air Division headquarters. PACAF directed the new wing to accomplish all tactical reconnaissance in SEA.[18]

PACAF also discontinued 2d Air Division on 1 April 1966 and organized and activated seventh Air Force in its stead. During the last 10 days of March, PACAF moved the 20th Tactical Reconnaissance Squadron and its RF-101s from Tan Son Nhut Air Base to Udorn RTAFB to replace the Green Python Task Force. The 15th Tactical Reconnaissance squadron personnel and aircraft that had made up the Green Python Task Force returned to Kadena Air Base after having flown 4,349 reconnaissance sorties and 6,786 flying hours in 1 year. The 45th Tactical Reconnaissance Squadron sent 12 RF-101Cs and crews to Tan Son Nhut Air Base to take over Able Mable responsibilities. All of the moves had been completed by 1 April, giving Seventh Air Force a squadron of RF-101Cs at Udorn RTAFB and a squadron of RF-4Cs, plus a detachment of RF-101Cs at Tan Son Nhut Air Base.[19]

Additional reorganization moves increased the strength of the reconnaissance force in mid-year. The 20th Tactical Reconnaissance Squadron at Udorn RTAFB found its 12 RF-101Cs inadequate to satisfy the growing reconnaissance requirements, so PACAF in May increased the squadron's authorized strength to 16 aircraft. The 15th Tactical Reconnaissance squadron quickly sent four of its Voodoos to bring the 20th up to strength. Four RF-101C's and crews also arrived at Udorn RTAFB from USAFE in July, at which time the 15th Tactical Reconnaissance Squadron moved four of its aircraft from Udorn RTAFB to Tan Son Nhut Air Base to augment the 45th Tactical Reconnaissance Squadron. On 23 July, PACAF moved all remaining aircraft and personnel of the 45th Tactical Reconnaissance squadron to Tan Son Nhut Air Base as Detachment 1. The squadron title and official headquarters remained at Misawa Air Base, Japan, with one officer and one airman. Scheduled to convert to RF-4Cs, the 15th Tactical Reconnaissance Squadron at Kadena Air Base became a replacement pool for RF-101Cs, delivering aircraft to SEA within 24 to 48 hours after a combat or operational loss.[20]

Although the reconnaissance force grew quite rapidly during .|965, the amount of film exposed increased even more rapidly. As mentioned earlier, the measure of reconnaissance success had been shifting from the intelligence yardstick of how many assigned objectives had been photographed on each mission to the operations measure of how many feet of film were exposed. However, it was the 2d Air Division Director of Intelligence, Brigadier General Rocky Triantafellu, who on 18 December 1965 established the policy that converted the measurement of reconnaissance success from intelligence production to film consumption. He ordered that whenever the weather conditions were favorable, reconnaissance pilots would keep their cameras running while over enemy territory. Once the primary and alternate objectives had been photographed, the pilots were to use all remaining film to photograph targets of opportunity or just whatever they happened to fly over. Miles of film rolled through the photo processing machines and across the photo interpreters light tables, and 2d Air Division could boast about the miles of aerial film its reconnaissance aircraft had exposed.[21] Repeated efforts by the intelligence staffs at 2d Air Division headquarters and PACAF to reverse this trend failed, and only a tiny percentage of the film could be exploited to produce intelligence. Meanwhile, changes to operational tactics made for better overall missions.

Damage to the RF-101Cs from antiaircraft fire diminished dramatically during November and December, with only one aircraft receiving a single hit on 8 November. The pilots gave much of the credit for the great improvement to an adaptation of the popup maneuver by Major Harry V. Runge of the 15th Tactical Reconnaissance Squadron. The maneuver called for a low-altitude, run to a point 5 miles from the high-speed objective, where the pilot cut in the afterburners and climbed to between 10,000 and 15,000 feet with the long focal length split-vertical cameras running. He crossed the target in level flight with the appropriate cameras turned on, and then dove back to the relative safety of very low altitudes. The popup had many advantages, not the least of which was its ability to frustrate gun and missile defenses while the RF-101Cs photographed their objectives and returned safely to base.[22]

As Christmas 1965 neared, President Johnson decided to call a holiday truce. His military advisers protested that such a truce could only work to the enemy's advantage, but the President apparently had made up his mind. The JCS planned an intensive reconnaissance program over North Vietnam during both the Christmas and New Year truces to determine how the North Vietnamese reacted. Their findings supported the military contention that the North Vietnamese were using the truces to improve significantly their situation. Thousands of people repaired and rebuilt roads, bridges, rail lines, and other essential facilities, not even running for cover when the RF-101Cs swept by. The President continued the bombing halt through the end of January 1966, hoping that the North Vietnamese would respond by agreeing to peace talks, but the enemy only intensified his reconstruction and resupply efforts. The North Vietnamese rebuilt or replaced dozens of road and rail bridges and built one or more bypasses for each of the more vital bridges. Long lines of trucks moved into Laos with enough materiel to keep the Viet Cong and North Vietnamese units in South Vietnam supplied with food and ammunition for many months. The Voodoos photographed the reconstruction and resupply effort whenever the seasonably poor weather permitted.[23]

Poor weather persisted over North Vietnam during the early months of 1966, producing the usual unsafe flying conditions. Most of the RF-101C pilots on reconnaissance missions into the area let down through the clouds over the open water of the Gulf of Tonkin, frequently breaking into the clear at altitudes of 200 feet or less. North Vietnamese radars acquired the Voodoos as they approached the letdown area at high altitudes and tracked them to their objectives. The pilots normally encountered intense automatic weapons and antiaircraft fire from the time they crossed the coast until they left North Vietnam. Whenever the cloudcover had holes, the pilots preferred to let down over land, despite the additional hazards. As the aircraft broke into the clear under the low cloudbase, the pilot had to orient himself quickly and turn to the best course to his initial point (IP). This required that he be able to recognize rivers, terrain features, and towns at a glance and have committed to memory every detail of his mission. If the pilot could not reach his IP because of poor weather, he aborted the mission.[24]

Despite the dangers and the growing threat, however, the RF-l0lCs brought back photography of great value. In January 1966, for instance, two RF-l0lCs piloted by Major Harry V. Runge and Captain Jerdy A. Wright, Jr., of the 15th Tactical Reconnaissance Squadron photographed a stretch of Highway I in the North Vietnam panhandle. At one point, the photography showed more than 30 trucks lined up to cross a temporary bridge and continue their journey to the south.[25]

Constantly growing enemy missile defenses also made life more difficult for the reconnaissance crews over Laos and North Vietnam. As early as January 1966, pilots reported probable SAM launches from points south of Vinh, even though the photo interpreters were unable to find the launch position. By mid February, electronic intercepts confirmed that SAM sites were operational as far south as Vinh and Dong Hoi, and the presence of such sites was further emphasized by an increased concentration of antiaircraft guns. In addition, ground fire increased dramatically in the Mu Gia, Nape, and Barthelemey passes and at other key road junctions.[26]

Voodoo Losses

As the threats multiplied, RF-l0lCs began to suffer losses. The Green Python Task Force suffered its first aircraft loss on 29 April 1965 when a pilot ejected after automatic weapons fire hit his RF-101C near Sam Neua, Laos. The pilot reportedly was seen on the ground several times over the next few days, but every recovery effort failed. The aircraft was quickly replaced from Kadena Air Base, but the pilot was listed as missing in action. On 22 May, a jammed rudder caused the RF-l0lC piloted by Lieutenant Colonel Raymond A. Lowery of the 363d

Tactical Reconnaissance Wing to crash on landing at Ubon RTAFB. The aircraft was a total loss, but the pilot emerged uninjured.[27] Anti-aircraft fire in the Phu Tho area on 29 July hit an RF-101C from the 45th Tactical Reconnaissance Squadron, causing it to explode. Antiaircraft fire also destroyed a 15th Tactical Reconnaissance Squadron RF-101C on a low-altitude, high-speed run between Phu Tho and Viet Tri on 13 August.[28]

Two RF-l0lCs departed Udorn RTAFB on 5 October 1965 to obtain BDA photography of the Long Met ammunition depot and a nearby bridge, both about 30 miles northeast of Hanoi. The pilots planned to cross their objectives about l5 minutes after the strike force dropped its bombs, at a time when the enemy defenses would be alerted and waiting. Kep Airfield, only 2 minutes flying time to the south, was the home of several MiG's, so the threat could come from above or below. A 3,000-foot cloud base held the Voodoos well within range of the antiaircraft guns and reduced their ability to outmaneuver the flak and missiles. Every factor favored the enemy, but the two pilots continued their mission.

About 8 miles from the objective, the two Voodoo pilots flashed over a low ridge. and ran into a well-placed antiaircraft barrage that damaged both aircraft. The lead aircraft, piloted by Captain Robert Pitt, broke into flames. Captain Pitt shut down the burning engine and the fire went out. He turned toward the Gulf of Tonkin, hoping to reach the water before ejecting. With a less seriously damaged aircraft, his wingman endured the intense antiaircraft fire for more than a minute to photograph both objectives, and then caught up with his leader. Within 30 miles of Da Nang Air Base and still flying, Captain Pitt decided to try to save his seriously damaged RF-l0lC.

As his aircraft staggered southward, Captain Pitt saw that he was critically short of fuel. Flak had torn his fuel cells to shreds, and he already had lost more than a ton of fuel. He was able to contact an Air Force tanker aircraft that flew north to his aid, but when he tried to take on fuel he discovered that the flak also had damaged his hydraulic system, and he could not open his refueling receptacle. Still l0 miles from the Da Nang runway, he had only 200 pounds of fuel remaining, but he continued on. Five miles from the base he used emergency procedures to lower the gear. The Voodoo lurched toward the side of the runway and the pilot worked the rudder pedals, but nothing happened. The enemy flak had destroyed his rudder controls, so Captain Pitt could only ride the slowing but uncontrolled Voodoo. Off the runway it went, shearing the landing gear and crashing through a radio shack before coming to a halt. Captain Pitt climbed from a demolished aircraft with only minor injuries. His wingman flew back to Udorn RTAFB with the costly film.[29]

Until then, antiaircraft fire had accounted for all RF-l0lC losses, but CINCPAC in early November 1965 expressed some concern that the MiGs represented an even greater potential threat to the unarmed reconnaissance aircraft. Headquarters 2d Air Division assured him that the Voodoos were highly maneuverable and capable of outrunning the MiG-l5 and MiG-l7 fighters that had been seen on North Vietnam's airfields.

Two RF-l0lC pilots on a reconnaissance mission 30 miles northwest of Hanoi on 15 November 1965 proved their ability to get out of a tight spot. Flying the usual loose formation on a northeasterly heading at 9,000 feet, the two RF-l0lCs were approximately 7 miles east of Yen Bay when the wingman spotted two MiGs passing behind them at 15,000 feet. Because the flight leader had begun his photo run and was concentrating on his navigation, he did not see the MiGs, even after his wingman reported them. As the MiGs dove on the leader, the wingman called to him to break and slid his aircraft between the leader and the MiGs. The enemy switched their attention to the wingman while the leader finished his photo run and broke down and away. Twisting and turning, the wingman found the nimble MIG's turning inside of him and gradually forcing him in the wrong direction. His fuel was nearing the critical point and it was time to stop maneuvering and use the Voodoo's superior speed. He slithered down to 500 feet, rolled out level on a heading toward the city of Yen Bay, and dove to 100 feet, virtually in the tree tops. As he streaked across the roofs of the city, every antiaircraft battery opened fire, but all were firing well behind the Voodoo. The MiGs thought better of flying through their own flak and broke off the pursuit. When the two undamaged RF-101Cs landed safely at Udorn RTAFB, the leader had brought back complete photography of their assigned objective.[30]

The MiG-17 was a nasty little beast but an RF-101C could easily outrun it.
Source: U.S. Air Force.

MiGs again tried to down two RF-101Cs on 26 November in the same general area. While flying a reconnaissance mission northeast of Yen Bay, two pilots spotted at least four MiGs diving on them. When the MiGs opened fire at a range of 4,000 feet, the Voodoo pilots broke sharply to the left and dove to about 200 feet, accelerating all the way and leveling off on a course for home base. They could no longer see the MiGs which apparently had broken off the attack. Even when outnumbered, the RF-101C appeared to be more than a match for the MiG-17.[31]

Two RF-l0lCs photographing objectives southwest of Hanoi on I January 1967 received an electronic warning that hostile aircraft were approaching. The Voodoos turned for home at once and gained the relative safety of Laos before the unidentified aircraft broke off at the Laotian border. Because of the high speed of the pursuers, the Voodoo pilots believed they were MiG-21s rather than the older and slower MIG-17s, but they were unable to make a visual identification. The dense cloudcover had hampered the RF-101Cs in their photographic work but on this occasion it also helped them elude the North Vietnamese MiGs.[32]

The MiG-21 was a much greater threat to the RF-101C flights.
Source: U.S. Air Force

Despite the growing menace of the MiGs, however, ground fire continued to take the greatest toll. Two Voodoo pilots assigned to photograph the Xuan Son Army barracks in North Vietnam on 26 January 1966 swept across their objectives through light automatic weapons fire and climbed into the bottom of the clouds at 1,500 feet. One of the pilots called that his aircraft had been hit, and never emerged from the top of the cloud layer at 5,000 feet. Navy A-1s and Air Force F-105s searched the area but failed to find the downed pilot. The North Vietnamese later reported that they had captured him.[33]

Automatic weapons fire on 21 March hit an RF-101C piloted by Captain Arthur Burer of the 45th Tactical Reconnaissance Squadron while he was flying between Vinh and Thanh Hoa along Route l at a very low altitude. Captain Burer pulled up and headed for the Gulf of Tonkin, but shortly thereafter the Voodoo burst into flames. The pilot ejected and landed without injury, but the North Vietnamese captured him. He was returned by the North Vietnamese in 1973. 0n 2 April 1966, another 45th pilot, Captain Daniel J. Doughty, was over North Vietnam on a reconnaissance mission when antiaircraft fire hit his RF-l0lC. He ejected, and the other RF-l0lC in the flight photographed his open parachute as it descended. Rescue attempts were not successful. Captain Doughty was captured and remained a prisoner until 1973.[34]

Fortunately, not all of the downed Voodoo pilots became prisoners. While on a low-altitude reconnaissance mission over the demilitarized zone (DMZ) on 4 November 1966, an RF-101C piloted by Captain Denis J. Haney took several hits from ground fire. Captain Haney turned his aircraft out over the water and ejected about 25 miles from shore. The 45th Tactical Reconnaissance Squadron pilot was in the water only 30 minutes before being rescued.[35]

On 8 February 1967, Captain John H. Rogers, Jr., of the 45th Tactical Reconnaissance Squadron was flying a special RF-l0lC mission over the Quang Khe ferry complex at 4,500 feet and 500 knots when antiaircraft fire ripped into his aircraft and set it afire. Captain Rogers nursed the crippled Voodoo out over the Gulf of Tonkin before ejecting and landing safely in the water. Several hostile junks and sampans headed for the pilot, but an A-l aircraft found him and drove off the watercraft with cannon fire. then the Navy destroyer Cunningham plucked Captain Rogers from the water 17 minutes later. He reported that trucks were traveling practically bumper to bumper along Highway I between Ron and Quang Khe.[36]

Although the loss of pilots and aircraft to ground fire was difficult to accept, it was even more disturbing when aircraft and crews simply disappeared. On 7 March 1966, two RF-l0lCs departed Udorn RTAFB to fly a low-altitude reconnaissance mission near Thanh Hoa. Shortly after crossing into North Vietnam, both aircraft disappeared. About the time the Voodoos were scheduled to photograph their first objective, the U.S.S. Berkeley, cruising in the Gulf of Tonkin, intercepted a radio message from an unidentified aircraft indicating that a SAM had destroyed another aircraft, but there was no identification for either aircraft. Search aircraft never found any wreckage, and the pilots have since been listed as killed in action.[37]

Lone aircraft were even more vulnerable to disappearing without a trace. Major William D. Burroughs on 31 July departed Udorn RTAFB in an RF-101C to fly a reconnaissance mission northwest of Hanoi and disappeared. This time there was not even a radio call to indicate that something had happened. When Burroughs was repatriated in 1973, he reported that 37mm rounds had hit his aircraft, forcing him to eject at about 500 feet AGL.[38]

Although any claims that the aircraft had been downed by SAMs would have been pure guesswork, there already was some definite evidence of the increasing missile threat. Flying a single aircraft mission, an RF-101C pilot on 22 May 1966 had photographed the Thai Nguyen railroad station, approximately 35 miles northwest of Hanoi, and had turned homeward at 4,000 feet when he saw a SAM headed toward him. He broke directly toward the flying white telephone pole, missing it by little more than 100 feet. He had not seen it launched and was so busy getting out of the area that he did not see it detonate.[39] Besides the SAMs, the pilots were also still dodging MiGs.

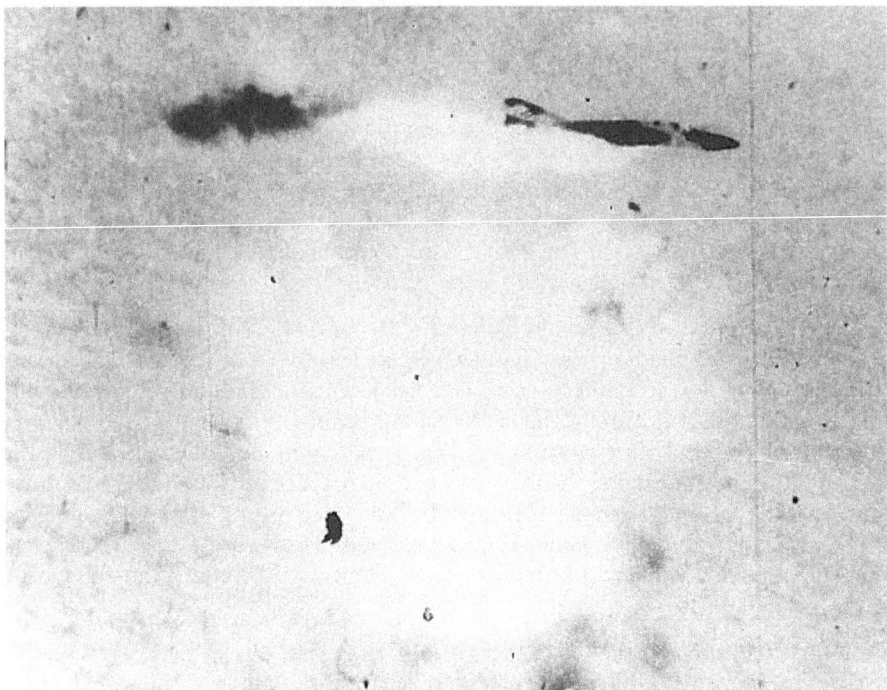

Reconnaissance aircraft (in this case an RF-4C) hit by an SA-2 Guideline missile. The fragments from the explosion have ruptured the aircraft's fuel tanks and the crew have only a few seconds left to eject. Capts. Edwin Atterberry and Thomas Parrott were captured after ejecting. Atterberry died in the hands of the North Vietnamese after an escape attempt and Parrott was released at the end of the war.

Source: U.S. Air Force

Two RF-101Cs piloted by Major Hallet P. Marston and Captain Richard M. Cooper were flying a reconnaissance mission near Dien Bien Phu in northwestern North Vietnam on 17 March 1966 when MiGs made four passes. Fortunately, the haze was so dense that the MiGs were not able to maintain visual contact, allowing the RF-101Cs to turn on afterburners and easily outdistance the pursuers without damage. A flight of two RF-101Cs over North Vietnam on 16 September 1966 were not so fortunate. The pilots had no inkling that MiGs were in the area until the wingman suddenly called that his aircraft had been hit. The leader saw that his wingman's aircraft was in flames, and suddenly realized that he also was under attack as two rounds detonated about 100 feet ahead of him. Before he ejected, the wingman called that the MiG was directly over them, but the leader never saw it.[40]

Such losses, whatever the cause, constituted a serious drain on the number of available Voodoos. The 15th Tactical Reconnaissance Squadron at Kadena Air Base delivered an RF-101C to SEA to replace each loss, but by the end of 1966 it had delivered the last of its aircraft. The Voodoo replacement pool was empty.[41]

Changes and Results

Seventh Air Force headquarters in mid-June 1966 made a change in reconnaissance tactics that increased aircraft availability but somewhat reduced pilot survivability. The new directive required that single RF-l0lCs fly missions into heavily defended portions of North Vietnam, replacing the standard two aircraft flights. A single aircraft presented a smaller and less inviting target, perhaps, and the pilot could concentrate on his own survival, but he had no friendly wingman to help whenever things went wrong. Shortly thereafter, on 29 June, Major Hallet P. Marston flew his RF-101C low across the burning Hanoi petroleum, oil and lubricants (POL) storage area to photograph the results of a strike by F-105's. The spectacular photography showed smoke billowing far above the reconnaissance aircraft.[42]

One of Major Marston's classic bomb damage assessment photographs.
Source: U.S. Air Force

Major Marston's photography of the Hanoi POL storage area was part of an aggressive reconnaissance program to cover all POL storage and handling facilities in North Vietnam. Nicknamed Blue Tree, the routine reconnaissance missions over North Vietnam provided prestrike photography for crew study and planning purposes, but Seventh Air Force headquarters scheduled BDA reconnaissance as part of each strike mission. All BDA was supposed to be accomplished within 36 hours after each strike giving the mission planners some flexibility in mission timing. The added workload increased the number of RF-101C missions by 10 per day, but by late August that increase proved to be totally inadequate as CINCPAC complained that there had been no BDA photography of at least 36 bombed targets. Without an evaluation, the planners could only schedule renewed bombing to insure that the POL storage facilities were indeed destroyed.[43] But post-strike BDA photography was just one of the uses of reconnaissance.

The Viet Tri POL storage area became a point of contention when the Defense Intelligence Agency (DIA) and PACAF headquarters disagreed on its residual storage capacity. The DIA estimated that the undamaged tanks could store 1,320 metric tonnes of POL, but the PACAF experts contended that the site could store only 325. RF-101C pilots procured high resolution photography of the installation, which the specialists used to carefully measure and appraise each remaining tank. PACAF headquarters and the DIA finally agreed that the true residual storage capacity was actually 43 metric tons.[44]

Voodoo photography also showed that the North Vietnamese were taking advantage of U.S. policies which the press forced into public debate. There had been a furor in the United States when the subject of bombing dikes was aired. The Red River had been diked for centuries and continued silting had built its bed above the surrounding land. Bombing of the dikes could have killed many thousands of people and destroyed vital farm land, homes, roads, and railroads. The United States, however, chose not to follow such a course and publicly stated that it would not bomb dikes or dams. Shortly thereafter, the RF-101Cs photographed POL storage tanks being buried in the dikes along the Song La River southwest of Vinh. It was the safest place for the POL, and the North Vietnamese were quick to take advantage of U.S. humanitarian concessions.[45]

Another squadron of RF-4Cs, the 12th Tactical Reconnaissance Squadron, arrived at Tan Son Nhut Air Base on 9 September 1966 to increase the base force to three reconnaissance squadrons. A complicated augmentation also added a squadron of RF-4Cs at Udorn RTAFB by October, and a series of designation changes resulted in the new unit becoming the 11th Tactical Reconnaissance Squadron. The geographical division of the reconnaissance force was strengthened in August when COMUSMACV learned that less than half of the sorties flown by reconnaissance aircraft at Tan Son Nhut Air Base covered objectives in Laos and South Vietnam. On 29 August therefore, he directed that the reconnaissance aircraft based in South Vietnam photograph only objectives in South Vietnam, the southern tip of Laos, and the southern portion of North Vietnam. The reconnaissance aircraft based at Udorn RTAFB could cover only objectives in northern Laos and North Vietnam. This appeased the MACV staff, but reduced the flexibility of the reconnaissance force.[46]

Because the added squadrons had increased the number of flying units subordinate to the 460th Tactical Reconnaissance Wing to nine, which exceeded the acceptable span of control, the Commander in Chief, Pacific Air Forces (CINCPACAF), again asked for permission to activate a tactical reconnaissance wing at Udorn RTAFB. He got it. With the requisite authority in hand, PACAF headquarters on 18 September organized the 432d Tactical Reconnaissance Wing to control all reconnaissance units in Thailand. The reconnaissance force then was divided geographically and by command, although Seventh Air Force headquarters exercised operational control.[47]

Despite military objections, President Johnson again announced a 2-day truce for Christmas 1966. Once again the RF-101C pilots braved the seasonably poor weather to photograph the swell of enemy activity that began the minute the truce went into effect. Large truck convoys sped openly along the roads during daylight hours and hundreds of watercraft plied the rivers, canals, and coastal waters. Another truce on 1 January produced the same general activity, as well as more aggressive defensive reaction by the North Vietnamese. Both were massive resupply efforts that took advantage of every safe minute.[48]

As the president allowed power plants, factories, and major bridges in North Vietnam to be bombed, General William N. Momyer, Seventh Air Force commander, came under greater pressure from Washington to hasten the evaluation of the bombing results. Because the aircraft from Udorn RTAFB flew most of the BDA reconnaissance missions over North Vietnam, photo interpretation reports and photographs of most key targets took many hours to reach General Momyer and his staff. To speed the reporting process, RF-101Cs which photographed high priority targets in North Vietnam frequently refueled from a tanker aircraft after coming out of North Vietnam and then landed at Tan Son Nhut Air Base. The photo laboratory processed their film immediately, and within a matter of minutes General Momyer had preliminary damage assessments and photographs. It was hard on the Voodoo pilots, who had to fly their refueled aircraft back to Udorn RTAFB to be readied for another mission, but it accelerated the intelligence cycle.[49]

President Johnson announced plans for a 5-day truce during the 1967 celebration of Tet, the lunar new year. Faced with yet another massive North Vietnamese resupply operation, CINCPAC directed that every available reconnaissance vehicle cover transportation facilities in North Vietnam and Laos. However, the reconnaissance aircraft could not fly below 12,000 feet on day missions without specific CINCPAC approval, despite the expected dense cloud cover and low ceilings.[50]

During the first 2 days of the Tet truce, RF-101Cs photographed more than 1,500 trucks along Route 15 northeast of Mu Gia Pass and along Route 1 north and south of Dong Hoi. At the Quang Khe ferry, 176 vessels and 14 barges busily off-loaded cargo. Despite reduced flying because of very poor weather throughout the final 3 days, the reconnaissance aircraft confirmed 2,799 trucks and 3,112 watercraft in the southern third of the panhandle of North Vietnam during the 5-day truce. On 9 February, RF-101Cs photographed tracked amphibious vehicles at Quang Khe; the next day two RF-101Cs photographed a Russian-made Mi-6 "Hook" helicopter on the Dien Bien Phu airfield -- apparently engaged in resupply operations. The evidence produced by aerial reconnaissance led Air Force intelligence analysts to estimate that during the 5-day truce the North Vietnamese had moved 800 truckloads of supplies per day, enough to support four Vietcong divisions with essential supplies for almost 4 years, or the North Vietnamese Army divisions then in South Vietnam and Laos for more than a year. [51]

Some truly spectacular photography came from special missions by RF-I01Cs over the panhandle of North Vietnam. A requirement for detailed information concerning coastal defenses resulted in one such mission. With a 24-inch focal length KA-1 camera mounted in the forward bay to take nose obliques a young pilot flew his RF-101C northward along the beach at tree-top level with the camera operating at its fastest cyclic rate. The weather was good, and people caught in the open appeared dumb-founded or terrified at the sight of the Voodoo that popped into sight without warning and was gone as quickly, leaving behind only the terrible noise of its passing. The photo interpreters were enthralled by the detail visible in the large, sharp photographs and wanted more missions of that type. Unfortunately, such missions had to be reserved for very special objectives because of the automatic weapons massed in that part of North Vietnam.

Although the Air Force placed the major emphasis on reconnaissance over North Vietnam, the RF-101Cs routinely continued to photograph objectives throughout South Vietnam. Most such objectives required mosaic-type photography of large areas, but occasionally a fleeting target or an emergency situation mandated a higher priority response. To meet such contingencies, at the beginning of each daily flying schedule seventh Air Force headquarters placed two RF-101Cs on alert at Tan Son Nhut Air Base, one for in-country emergencies and the other for contingencies in Laos or North Vietnam. If no high priority requirements arose within 3 or 4 hours, the pilots flew a routine reconnaissance sortie while other RF-101Cs and pilots assumed the alert status.

When an RF-101C discovered and photographed a truck convoy moving through the Mu Gia Pass into Laos on 20 February 1967, for instance, the RF-101C on alert status scrambled from Tan Son Nhut Air Base maintained surveillance until strike aircraft bombed the convoy, and then photographed the results. Other similar sorties proved the value of the RF-101C in covering such fleeting targets in Laos and South Vietnam.[52]

Both before and after the Tet truce, a JCS campaign against the railroad system in North Vietnam required daily tactical reconnaissance of all major rail lines. Several reconnaissance sorties preceded each major strike mission against railroad segments, and at least one BDA mission followed. Photography of the Thai Nguyen railroad station and yards, largest in North Vietnam and railhead for the nearby iron and steel complex, showed that the energetic North Vietnamese kept at least one through rail Line operational most of the time in spite of the repeated bombings.[53]

Weather conditions gradually improved over North Vietnam during April and May 1967, particularly along the north-east railroad between Hanoi and the China border, the segment where strike missions then were concentrating. Two RF-101C pilots in that area on 22 May 1967 photographed 25 assigned objectives, 25 bonus objectives, and an 80-nautical-mile strip to the Gulf of Tonkin. That same day another RF-l0lC pilot, jinking to avoid more than 20 missiles ripple-fired at his aircraft from the Hanoi defenses, photographed a perfect dispersion pattern of the approximately 3,600 warhead fragments of a missile that detonated about 200 feet from his camera.[54] Fortunately, his aircraft escaped damage and he brought back the photographs.

By mid-1967, the RF-101C pilots had reached the peak of their SEA operations. They were active over all of North Vietnam and brought back excellent photography of a wide variety of objectives. Their large format, long focal length cameras provided specialized coverage not available from other reconnaissance vehicles. The Voodoos were old and well-worn, but they also were dependable and highly acclaimed.

President Richard M Nixon. Source: U.S. National Archives

President Lyndon B Johnson. Source: U.S. National Archives

General William Wallace Momyer was born in 1916 and entered the USAAF in 1938. He was assigned to pilot and flight commander duties until February 1941, when be became military observer for air with the military attaché in Cairo, Egypt. In July 1966, he went to Vietnam to serve as deputy commander for air operations, Military Assistance Command, Vietnam, and also, commander, 7th Air Force. He served in this role until August 1968, at which time he assumed command of Tactical Air Command. General Momyer retired in 1973.
Source: U.S. Air Force

Lieutenant General Joseph H. Moore (1914 - 2006) joined the USAAF in June 1937. When World War II started he was in the Philippine Islands, and by April 1942 he had flown 100 combat hours in P-40 fighter aircraft. In January 1964 he became commander of the Second Air Division in Vietnam. On April 1, 1966, the 7th Air Force was reactivated and took over the duties formerly assigned to Second Air Division in Southeast Asia. General Moore remained as commander. General Moore retired in 1971.
Source: U.S. Air Force

General William C. Westmoreland (1914 - 2005) entered West Point in 1932. Following graduation in 1936, he became an artillery officer and served in several commands. In World War II he saw combat in Tunisia, Sicily, France and Germany. In June 1964, he became deputy commander of Military Assistance Command, Vietnam (MACV), assuming direct control from General Paul D. Harkins. He retained this position until being replaced by General Creighton Abrams in June 1968, the decision being announced s after the Tet Offensive.
Source: U.S. Army

CHAPTER IV .. DECLINE: AND WITHDRAWAL

By mid-1967, the RF-l0lC was 10 years old and had seen hard usage in SEA. As one might expect, parts wore out with increasing frequency and maintenance problems became more serious. Probably the most significant problem was the declining quality of the J-57 engines, many of which came back from depot overhaul facilities with more defects than before. Despite intensified efforts by maintenance personnel equipment failure caused the loss of some RF-101Cs.

0n 7 July 1967, for example, as a pilot from the 45th Tactical Reconnaissance Squadron departed Tan Son Nhut Air Base on a routine reconnaissance mission, the hydraulic system in his RF-101 failed around 5,000 feet AGL. He flew to the tank jettison area, dropped his full tanks, and then proceeded toward Tan Son Nhut Air Base at 5,000 feet, burning off excess fuel. When the right engine fire warning light came on, the pilot shut down the engine and lined up for a straight-in approach. The pilot throttled back the left engine when its fire warning light blinked on. Without further warning that engine flamed out, and when he was unable to restart either engine, the pilot ejected. Although there was some conjecture that Viet Cong small arms fire might have damaged the aircraft on takeoff or in the jettison area, Seventh Air Force headquarters attributed the loss to "operational factors." This was a generic term used to indicate an unknown or unproven factor associated with materiel failure, mechanical malfunction, fuel starvation, collision, atmospheric conditions, or similar cause related to some aspect of the in-flight operation of an aircraft.

RF-101 Crash. Source U.S. Air Force

The squadron lost another RF-101C on 26 July 1967 under very similar circumstances, and again Seventh Air Force headquarters listed operational factors as the probable cause.[1] Other operational losses resulted from the incredibly dense air traffic over South Vietnam, particularly near the major air bases and the larger Army ground operations. 0n 9 August, an RF-l0lC on a reconnaissance sortie over South Vietnam collided with an Army UH-lD Huey helicopter. The mixture of high speed jet aircraft and slow helicopters in a small airspace produced a volatile flying safety atmosphere.[2]

Because many new reconnaissance pilots were encountering such unsafe conditions for the first time, the 45th Tactical Reconnaissance Squadron planned indoctrination programs to insure maximum survivability. To check on their general proficiency and to keep the newer RF-l0lC pilots out of serious trouble, an instructor pilot flew a modified chase position with them on their first two reconnaissance sorties over South Vietnam. The new pilots then flew l0 additional reconnaissance sorties over South Vietnam before they were eligible for their first sortie outside South Vietnam. An instructor pilot again accompanied them on their first sortie over Laos or North Vietnam, and on their first aerial refueling mission.[3]

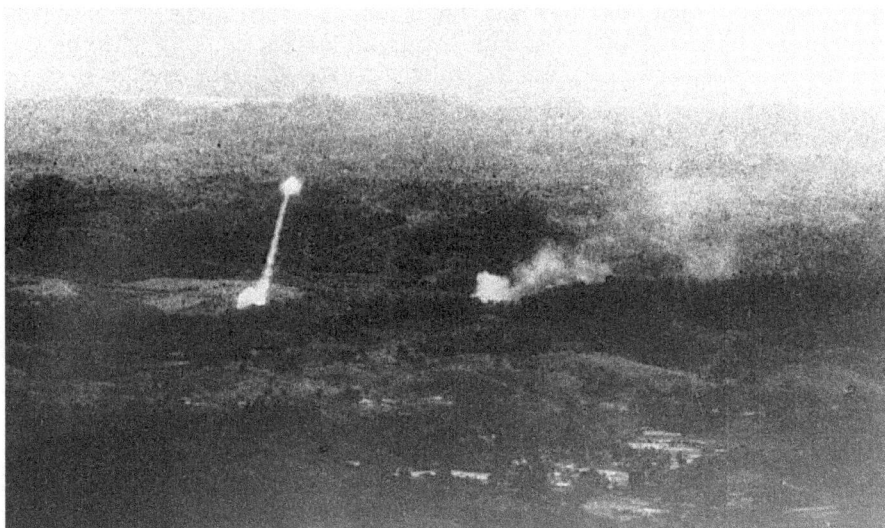

A Pair of SA-2 Missiles Launched: Source: U.S. Air Force

Even though the pilots were well indoctrinated, they were operating the RF-l0lC beyond safe limits. Because of its age, the Voodoo did not have the latest electronic defensive equipment and thus was not able to counter many of North Vietnam's SAM tactics. Inefficient handling of reconnaissance film by Air Force units further complicated the problem. A SAM destroyed an RF-l0lC about 40 miles southwest of Hoa Binh on 21 June 1967, and the North Vietnamese unsuccessfully launched five more missiles against the search and recovery aircraft that picked up the pilot. The photo interpreters had not reported any missiles in that area, but photography from a reconnaissance mission flown on the next day revealed an unoccupied site. Careful examination of 18 June photography showed that the site had been occupied, and that another site nearby also held missiles and support equipment. The North Vietnamese had set up their missiles in a basic, unimproved position, launched against the first good target, and run. Had the photo interpreters been able to exploit the photography of 18 June completely and quickly, their reports might have alerted the RF-l0lC pilot to the danger, and he could have made appropriate changes in his mission plan.[4]

Another missile downed an RF-l0lC on 1 August 1967, even though the Voodoo carried operational ALQ-51 deception jammers. Seventh Air Force headquarters, having suspected for some time that the ALQ-51 pods were ineffective against increasingly sophisticated radars in North Vietnam, withdrew them from use. As a substitute, it directed that the RF-l0lC pilots again fly in two-ship formations over North Vietnam, each aircraft carrying two ALQ-71 jamming pods originally designed for fighter aircraft. Because the large external pods reduced the RF-l0lC's speed and limited its maneuverability, making the aircraft easy prey for MiG's, Seventh Air Force headquarters directed that they avoid those areas where the MiGs were most active. An alternate procedure on some missions provided an escort of fighters carrying the ALQ-71 pods. 0n 22 August, for instance two escorted RF-l0lC pilots from Udorn RTAFB photographed four bridges in the Lang Son area of North Vietnam with long focal length cameras without seeing a missile launch or a MiG. When a MiG shot down another RF-l0lC on 16 September, however, Seventh Air Force headquarters directed that the Voodoos not be scheduled for reconnaissance missions over northern North Vietnam.[5]

The Ho Chi Minh Trail
Source: Vietnamese People's
Liberation Army

There remained plenty of reconnaissance work over Laos and the panhandle of North Vietnam for the Udorn-based RF-101Cs, and those based at Tan Son Nhut Air Base had far more requirements than they could handle. For some time the operations staff personnel at Seventh Air Force headquarters had espoused the idea of sending reconnaissance squadrons and detachments to other bases in South Vietnam to shorten response time and to accelerate the delivery of photographs, but intelligence staff personnel and General Momyer had opposed the idea. In August 1967, however, General Momyer allowed the 460th Tactical Reconnaissance Wing to begin a partial test of the concept. The 45th Tactical Reconnaissance Squadron readied 17 WS-430B vans -- expandable trailers containing processing and exploitation equipment -- for shipment to Phu Cat Air Base. Seventh Air Force units completed the airlift of the vans and requisite supplies and equipment--450,000 pounds in all—on 28 August 1967, and Forward Operating Location Alpha (FOLA) was fully operational by 3 September. [6]

Reconnaissance pilots from Tan Son Nhut Air Base photographed objectives in the northern provinces of South Vietnam and landed their aircraft at Phu Cat Air Base. The OLM personnel unloaded and processed the exposed film, reloaded the cameras, and refueled the aircraft. The pilots then took off from Phu Cat Air Base, photographed additional objectives, and landed at Tan Son Nhut Air Base. Seventh Air Force headquarters had to arrange for the airlift of more than 35,000 pounds of supplies to Phu Cat Air Base each month, but the operations staff was pleased with the experiment. Although the delivery of mission products continued to be too slow, the added base had speeded up the process because Phu Cat was close to many large Army units. The detachment worked well and seemed to prove the validity of the dispersal of reconnaissance assets. [7]

Some of the first missions turned around at Phu Cat Air Base were part of an operation nicknamed Neutralize, intended to find and destroy enemy artillery pieces in and above the DMZ that were battering the Marine positions south of the zone. Seventh Air Force headquarters launched the operation on 11 September 1967 with RF-4C reconnaissance sorties at medium altitude, but the photo interpreters were unable to find a single gun position on the photography. Seventh Air Force headquarters then scheduled a low altitude RF-101C mission over the area with the KA-l large format cameras. This time the photo interpreters found numerous gun positions, some with guns, and passed the target data to the Marine artillery and Air Force strike units. RF-101C pilots flew almost all of the subsequent missions at low altitude, photographing many artillery positions before Seventh Air Force headquarters ended the operation on 31 October. Despite intense counterbattery fire and numerous bombing missions, the photography from the many RF-l0lC BDA reconnaissance missions was unable to verify the destruction of a single enemy artillery piece. [8]

The Electronic Barrier

Secretary of Defense Robert S. McNamara on 15 September 1966 had ordered the development and installation of an anti-infiltration barrier intended to detect trucks and people moving through the DMZ or down that portion of the Ho Chi Minh Trail in Laos. Acoustic and seismic sensors planted adjacent to roads and trails transmitted signals of passing vehicles or people to a computer at Nakhon Phanom RTAFB, where specialists analyzed the data and developed targets. Work on the new system proceeded very rapidly and by August 1967 the barrier personnel were requesting increasing numbers of reconnaissance missions. Because they needed the photography for planning the location of sensor strings, the photo interpreters frequently specified RF-l0lCs for the low altitude missions. The KA-1 large format, split vertical cameras produced much sharper photography than the RF-4C cameras, even at altitudes of 300 to 500 feet AGL. Bad weather slowed the operation, but when the weather cleared on 18 and 19 0ctober, the RF-101Cs flew a total of 39 missions. By 31 October, the project was essentially complete. [9]

Even after the initial requirements had been satisfied, however, the workload continued to increase. The planners asked for photography of additional areas where sensors might be placed, and required that about 25 of the original areas be rephotographed monthly. In addition, RF-l0lC pilots had to photograph every sensor implant mission to record the exact sensor position. By the end of 1967, Seventh Air Force headquarters had committed almost the entire RF-101C force to supporting the electronic barrier, scheduling an average of five missions per day.[10]

As the reconnaissance workload increased, the RF-101C force decreased. Air Force headquarters told PACAF that it had shipped the last available RF-101C replacement to SEA in July 1967, and there were no more Voodoos anywhere in PACAF. 0n 31 October, PACAF deactivated the 20th Tactical Reconnaissance Squadron at Udorn RTAFB and transferred all but four of its aircraft and most of its people to the 45th Tactical Reconnaissance Squadron at Tan Son Nhut Air Base. By thus concentrating all of its. RF-l0lC's, PACAF generally limited them to reconnaissance missions over South Vietnam, the lower panhandle of Laos, and the southern tip of the panhandle of North Vietnam.[11]

Even with the smaller force, reduced operating areas, and lowered risks, maintenance and supply problems continued to increase. Replacement parts for the aged aircraft became more difficult to obtain as the depots used up stocks. Between 0ctober and December 1967, the base supply facility at Tan Son Nhut Air Base for no known reason reduced all RF-101C parts records to zero and threw away the stock cards. As new RF-l0lC parts arrived, the computer showed no need for them and supply personnel placed them aboard the next ship en route to the United States. By the time the 460th Tactical Reconnaissance Wing discovered what had been done, it was almost too late to recover. They reestablished the stock records at base supply and submitted emergency requisitions for the more critical parts, but almost 6 months passed before the parts stock again reached a satisfactory level. Meanwhile, a few RF-l0lCs were cannibalized to keep the others flying. It had been a costly supply error. [12]

President Johnson again ordered truce periods for Christmas and New Year, despite continued military opposition. CINCPAC once more directed intensified reconnaissance during the truce periods, with particular emphasis on the roads and waterways from Thanh Hoa southward through the panhandle. CINCPAC hoped to identify truck parks, supply storage areas, off-loading points, and similar logistics targets that U.S. aircraft could attack when the truce ended. Persistent cloud cover precluded photography of the lower panhandle during both truce periods, but low altitude visual reconnaissance revealed another logistic triumph for the North Vietnamese. [13]

Khe Sanh and Tet

Late in 1967 more than two divisions of regular North Vietnamese Army troops surrounded Khe Sanh, an isolated Marine outpost in the northwestern corner of South Vietnam. Faced with the choice of evacuating or defending, General W.C. Westmoreland, COMUSMACV, decided to defend the base despite apparently overwhelming odds. He directed that every intelligence agency use all of its assets to: measure the enemy strength, map enemy force dispositions, and evaluate probable enemy intentions. The RF-101C pilots joined other reconnaissance crews in photographing the Khe Sanh Valley many times over with every available type of camera. Unprecedented amounts of intelligence poured into MACV, where the staff went ahead with plans to support and defend the Marines at Khe Sanh.[14]

As the Khe Sanh defenses stiffened, North Vietnamese and Viet Cong forces launched an attack on cities and military bases throughout South Vietnam in the first few minutes of 31 January 1968. The assault wave burst across Tan Son Nhut Air Base and mortar rounds and rockets damaged several RF-101Cs. As soon as the engineers cleared and repaired the runway and security forces drove off the hostile troops, the pilots began flying missions with the serviceable RF-101Cs. Commanders throughout South Vietnam called for immediate aerial reconnaissance; the Voodoos had plenty of objectives to photograph that afternoon. [15]

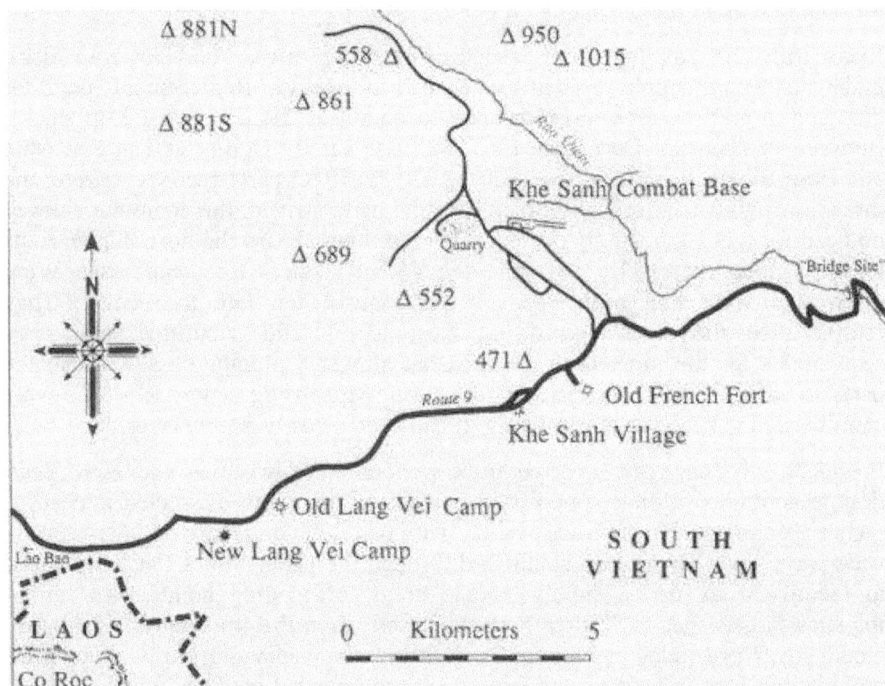

Khe Sanh and Lang Vei. Source: U.S. Marine Corps.

When intelligence sources indicated that at least one battered North Vietnam Army division was withdrawing from Khe Sanh in early February, General Westmoreland told General Momyer to use his reconnaissance aircraft to follow the departing unit. The North Vietnamese dealt another blow to the reconnaissance force at 0100 on 18 February, however, when their forces around Saigon launched several 122mm rockets against Tan Son Nhut Air Base. Among the casualties were one RF-101C destroyed and eight damaged. In a further fruitless search, the remaining RF-l0lCs photographed every inch of land around Saigon out to the maximum range of the rockets. Because those rockets used the simplest possible launching devices and left almost no trace, the photo interpreters could only select possible launch sites. The rockets kept coming, but their damage gradually diminished and no more RF-l0lCs were lost.[16]

As the defense of Khe Sanh came to a successful end, the reconnaissance sorties shifted to a variety of other high priority objectives within South Vietnam. RF-l0lC pilots in late March 1968 photographed enemy construction activity along Route 547 in the A Shau Valley, braving increasingly intense antiaircraft defenses. The pilots also photographed the tri-border area to develop intelligence data on current infiltration routes which soon became the targets for a series of Army operations: Grand Canyon, Buffalo, Truscott White, and Athens. The Voodoo pilots continued regular photographic coverage of the Saigon area to maintain a current enemy order of battle and to monitor suspected rocket launch sites and probable mortar positions. They also supported special operations, such as the week-long siege, evacuation, and destruction of the Kham Duc Special Forces Camp. Requests for the photography from the large format KA-l split vertical cameras kept the remaining Voodoos busy. [17]

Meanwhile, the RF-l0lC pilots continued to support the electronic barrier by flying about five missions per day over Laos to update the photo coverage and to photograph additional areas. Even after the intelligence specialists at Nakhon Phanom RTAFB became proficient at analyzing the signals to develop targets, the rules of engagement required visual or photographic confirmation of the target before bombing it. The RF-l0lC pilots successfully photographed suspected truck parks, bivouac areas, and similar fixed installations to develop strike targets, but the truck convoys were too fleeting. The electronic sensors had proven their ability to develop valid targets, but General Momyer and other commanders apparently had no confidence in their product. Truck convoys moved almost unmolested along the roads of Laos, even though the electronic sensors knew where they were.[18]

President Johnson went on television on 31 March 1968 to announce that all attacks against North Vietnam would halt at 0800 on I April, Saigon time, "except 'in the area north of the demilitarized zone, where the continuing enemy buildup directly threatens allied forward positions and where the movement of their troops and supplies are clearly related to that threat." He made no mention of aerial reconnaissance, but later decided that he needed surveillance of North Vietnam until both sides could agree to some form of control mechanism. Restricted as they were to the area just above the DM, the RF-l0lC pilots were little affected by the new rules of engagement. The North Vietnamese, however, took the United States at its word and began moving antiaircraft weapons and missiles southward into the lower panhandle. The threat to the RF-l0lCs and other U.S. aircraft increased rapidly as the number of occupied defense positions mounted.[19]

Voodoo pilots also participated in Operation Turnpike, designed to find and destroy North Vietnamese truck parks, supply depots, and bivouac areas along the infiltration routes. Lasting from 19 to 30 April 1968, it used all sources of intelligence but emphasized carefully interpreted photo imagery. Seventh Air Force headquarters told the photo interpreters to look for signs of enemy activity that appeared after strikes on particular targets. Trail and track activity, remains of structures, burned spots on the ground, explosion scars on foliage, and similar signs could verify the existence of fixed facilities that subsequently could be bombed. Again, the large format, long focal length cameras in the RF-10lCs provided the best possible photography.[20] Because Operation Turnpike was so successful, Seventh Air Force headquarters extended it through 25 June.

The Second Offensive

Bloodied badly in the Tet offensive, the Viet Cong and North Vietnamese forces still retained sufficient strength and resources for at least one more major assault. During April 1968, the RF-10lC pilots repeatedly photographed the Saigon area out to the l22mm rocket range, hoping to find rockets or launch sites before an assault began. When the attack came, however, it was almost as complete a surprise as the Tet offensive had been.

North Vietnamese 122mm rocket artillery battery. Finding dispersed sites like these was extremely difficult. 122mm rockets were responsible for the only RF-101C destroyed on the ground.

Source: Vietnamese People's Liberation Army.

In the first few minutes of 5 May, the North Vietnamese launched rocket and mortar attacks and ground assaults against cities and military installations throughout South Vietnam to initiate the long awaited second offensive. As the nightly attacks continued, the 460th Tactical Reconnaissance Wing flew five RF-10lCs to Phu Cat Air Base each evening to escape the rocket and mortar rounds. The aircraft returned to Tan Son Nhut Air Base the next morning, ready to fly normal daily reconnaissance sorties. The enemy apparently had planned for such a contingency, launching rockets into Phu Cat Air Base on the night of 11 May. The rockets damaged two of the RF-101Cs causing Seventh Air Force headquarters to cancel further nightly flights.[21]

Even as the enemy offensive slowly ground to a halt, rumors that the enemy could renew the offensive in June caused the alert to continue. The RF-10lCs continued to photograph 23 sensitive objectives near Saigon and the "rocket belt" around the city. Despite all of the concentrated effort, the enemy showed no indication of a renewed offensive, and the number of reconnaissance missions gradually returned to normal.[22]

Small arms fire continued to damage the RF-l0lCs, particularly in South Vietnam. To reduce the number of such incidents, the 460th Tactical Reconnaissance Wing in June 1968 established new policies governing reconnaissance mission planning. In heavily defended areas, the RF-l0lCs could make only a single pass over pinpoint objectives or road segments. The wing recommended a minimum altitude of 2,000 feet AGL for objectives in South Vietnam and Laos; in those areas where small arms fire was encountered most frequently, it suggested an altitude of 3,000 feet. If cloud cover forced the pilots to fly lower than those altitudes when photographing large areas, they could fly only three flight lines. The pilot had final discretion in each case, but the recommendations were a forceful guide. [23]

Although the workload diminished in South Vietnam, it picked up in Laos. The end of the monsoon cleared the rainy skies over the Ho Chi Minh Trail and the 1968 summer interdiction campaign officially began on 14 July. The RF-l0lC and RF-4C pilots photographed 19 carefully chosen interdiction points at least once each day, and usually much more often than that. Strike activity blocked the roads until the weather again turned bad in October. By 4 November, the North Vietnamese had repaired all of the roads leading into the Mu Gia and Ban Karai passes and were pushing large truck convoys through the mountains. Illustrative of the enemy rush to move supplies down the trail, an RF-l0lC pilot that day photographed a 40-truck convoy just east of the Mu Gia pass.[24]

Although the RF-101C pilots flew only a few sorties over North Vietnam just above the DMZ, those sorties overflew many SAM and antiaircraft gun positions, and losses were inevitable. Major Giles D. Harlow of the 45th Tactical Reconnaissance Squadron flew on such a mission on 6 August 1968 and ran into intense antiaircraft fire not far north of the DMZ. He saw tracers passing his aircraft before he felt a projectile hit somewhere behind the cockpit. When the hydraulic pressure on both control systems began fluctuating and the cockpit filled with smoke, Major Harlow turned toward the Gulf of Tonkin. At 20,000 feet the RF-l0lC suddenly pitched down, but the pilot regained control and continued toward the safety of the water. When the aircraft again pitched down and the controls froze, Major Harlow ejected. He suffered minor injuries from wind blast and the opening shock of the parachute, but landed safely in the water. A rescue helicopter picked him up almost at once.[25]

North Vietnamese heavy artillery again pounded U.S. and South Vietnamese positions below the DMZ in September causing Seventh Air Force to launch an informal reconnaissance program nicknamed Operation Foxtrot. Once again the RF-101C pilots thoroughly photographed the region from the southern edge of the DMZ to Bat Lake, searching for artillery positions and guns. The photo interpreters examined thousands of photographs, but found only four artillery pieces. Many more were hidden under the jungle canopy or concealed by excellent camouflage, and the shells continued to fall on the friendly positions south of the DMZ.[26]

Another maintenance crisis developed when the mechanics discovered that the potting compound in the electrical connectors of aircraft in SEA was melting and running out, leaving the wires exposed. Since the compound was intended as insulation and protection for the wires, its loss represented a hazardous situation. Fortunately, on the RF-101Cs only the wiring installed as part of the Project 1181 modification was affected. Rather than take the small force of Voodoos out of action to repair the damage, the Air Force sent a 16-man team to Tan Son Nhut Air Base to do the work. Working 7 long days each week, the team completed the repairs in less than a month.[27]

The Bombing Halt

President Johnson on 31 October told the nation that " . . . I have now ordered that all air, naval, and artillery bombardment of North Vietnam cease as of 8 a.m. Washington time Friday morning." When the U.S. negotiators went to Paris for peace talks, their instructions included a sentence that read: "The U.S. intends to continue reconnaissance flights, and the record should not preclude such flights." Again, the president had permitted continued reconnaissance over North Vietnam, but the RF-101C operating area remained virtually unchanged.[28]

Because of the uncertainty over North Vietnamese reaction to U.S. reconnaissance, the Air Force proceeded very cautiously, at first using only RF-4Cs for tactical reconnaissance missions north of the DMZ. Pilots from the 45th Tactical Reconnaissance Squadron flew five escorted RF-101C sorties just north of the DMZ on 3 December, all of which returned safely to base with good photography. The Voodoo pilots thereafter flew occasional daytime missions in the area, but were highly vulnerable. Until a more definite pattern of North Vietnamese reaction emerged, the Air Force kept such missions to a minimum.

On 20 December 1968, the RF-101C pilots began flying two sorties per day in support of Project Mac See, photographing selected interdiction targets in the A Shau Valley of northwestern South Vietnam. The photography confirmed suspicions that the North Vietnamese were using the main infiltration route through the valley, pushing men and supplies toward the coast. Each time U.S. or VNAF strike aircraft cut the road the enemy immediately made repairs and the infiltration flow continued. When three small caliber rounds hit a reconnaissance aircraft, Seventh Air Force set a minimum altitude of 2,500 feet AGL over the A Shau Valley for all reconnaissance aircraft.[30] Although this somewhat diminished the effectiveness of the cameras, the long focal length M-1 cameras in the RF-101Cs continued to produce big, clear photographs of the valley, allowing the photo interpreters to more accurately assess the magnitude of the infiltration flow.

The quickening tempo of the interdiction campaign in Laos mandated the best available photography of selected objectives, including the roads and trails over which the troops and supplies flowed toward South Vietnam. Each day from 29 January through 6 February 1969, two pilots of the 45th Tactical Reconnaissance Squadron launched their RF-101Cs from Tan Son Nhut Air Base, photographed designated roads, waterways, and other infiltration objectives with their M-1 cameras, and landed at Udorn RTAFB. Personnel of the 432d Tactical Reconnaissance Wing removed the exposed film for immediate processing and exploitation and reloaded the cameras so the RF-101C pilots could complete another reconnaissance mission on their return flight to Tan Son Nhut Air Base.[31]

Because of North Vietnamese defensive reactions to the continuing reconnaissance missions, fighters escorted all reconnaissance aircraft north of the DMZ. Seventh Air Force headquarters felt this needlessly hampered the RF-101C pilots in their missions below 17°15'N., a relatively low threat environment as long as the Voodoos remained above 15,000 feet. On 4 March 1969, therefore, Seventh Air Force headquarters asked that PACAF allow RF-101C pilots to fly unescorted reconnaissance missions over North Vietnam as far north as 17°15'N to photograph large areas and to maintain surveillance of Routes 1A and 101. PACAF on 8 March agreed, provided all RF-101Cs remained above 15,000 feet. Seventh Air Force headquarters found such a restriction acceptable because the 36-inch focal length KA-1 cameras took excellent photographs at a good scale from the higher altitudes.[32]

North Vietnamese antiaircraft defenses in the panhandle of Laos also grew dramatically in the early weeks of 1969. Intelligence sources estimated that at least 9,000 North Vietnamese Army regular troops manned 550 or more antiaircraft guns of all calibers in positions from Mu Gia Pass southward. When Operation Search began on 1 February, Air Force pilots flew RF-101Cs and RF-4Cs at 500 feet AGL at very high speeds along Routes 9 and 126 leading into the A Shau Valley of South Vietnam, searching for trucks, supply depots, truck parks, and other infiltration targets. By the time the operation ended on 7 April, the pilots had located 160 targets.[33]

Even though Air Force headquarters repeatedly had claimed that it could furnish no more RF-101C replacements, it occasionally shipped aircraft to Tan Son Nhut Air Base. Two RF-101Cs from Shaw Air Force Base reached Tan Son Nhut Air Base on 29 March 1969, and another arrived on 31 March. Although losses to enemy action diminished sharply, losses from other causes gradually reduced the force size. On 30 April, for example, as an instructor pilot in an RF-101C joined a newly assigned pilot in another RF-101C, the two collided. The pilots landed safely at Phu Cat Air Base, but both aircraft suffered extensive damage. The force lost the two aircraft for 2 weeks for repairs.[34]

One factor that once had reduced the effective force was the frequent and time-consuming change of camera configuration. By early 1969, the 45th Tactical Reconnaissance Squadron, with approval from higher headquarters, had eliminated much of that delay by standardizing the camera configuration of all of its RF-101Cs. A 12-inch focal length KS-72 camera in the nose compartment produced nose oblique photographs, particularly effective on the very infrequent dicing missions. A 3-inch focal length panoramic camera and a pair of 6-inch focal length KS-724's in a split vertical configuration filled the next camera compartment. All used narrow film to produce small format negatives. In the aft camera compartment were the two 36-inch KA-1 cameras in a split vertical mount. No matter what the requirement, some combination of those cameras almost always produced a satisfactory product.[35]

Some of the electronic equipment in the RF-101Cs also changed or improved during 1969. Between July and September, the Air Force added "Seek Silence" secure communications equipment to all RF-101Cs in SEA to make it possible for the pilots to radio urgent intelligence information to ground terminals without fear of the enemy intercepting their transmissions. The Air Force also equipped some of the RF-101Cs with high frequency (HF) sideband radios to improve communications. Depot teams installed both pieces of equipment at Tan Son Nhut Air Base as part of scheduled periodic maintenance. [36]

Seventh Air Force headquarters had preferred that the missions over the panhandle of North Vietnam be unescorted, but intensified antiaircraft defenses and the growing threat of MiG intervention precluded such operations. The RF-101C pilots on 20 June 1969 began flying one special escorted mission each day into the panhandle of North Vietnam, searching for SAMs, transshipment points, new roads, and similar targets. F-4E and F-105 aircraft provided escort, prepared to attack missile sites or gun positions. By September, the RF-101C pilots also were flying a daily unescorted sortie that remained south of 17°15'N to search for infiltration targets and SAM sites.[37]

Antiaircraft fire that hit the left wing of an RF-101C on 28 October set the aircraft afire, destroyed the utility hydraulic system, and caused the loss of left aileron control. The pilot managed to fly the crippled aircraft back to base, but was unable to lower his flaps to land. He touched down at a very high speed and blew both tires on the main landing gear, causing the RF-101C to leave the runway. The right main gear sheared, causing extensive damage to the right wing, but the pilot emerged uninjured.[33]

By the final quarter of 1969, a national economy trend was affecting the reconnaissance force in SEA. The operating location at Phu Cat Air Base turned around its last reconnaissance mission aircraft on 13 October 1969, shipped its equipment and personnel to the 45th Tactical Reconnaissance Squadron at Tan Son Nhut Air Base, and officially closed on 28 October 1969. Aerial refueling for RF-101Cs on missions into the northern provinces of South Vietnam had stretched their photography time considerably, but a drastic reduction in the number of refueling sorties in an economy drive to save fuel eliminated aerial refueling for reconnaissance aircraft. On the longer missions, the RF-101C pilots had to land at Da Nang Air Base for ground refueling, significantly lengthening the total mission time and delaying film processing several hours. Air Force headquarters also reduced the RF-101C crew ratio from 1.35 pilots per aircraft to 1.2 -- sending a number of pilots home early and canceling several replacements.[39]

Commando Hunt III

Commando Hunt III, the northeast monsoon interdiction campaign in Laos, began in October while the economy moves were reducing the capability of the reconnaissance force. The RF-101C pilots flew a few missions each week in support of Commando Hunt III, but were not deeply involved at first. New strike aircraft, exotic munitions, and aggressive tactics resulted in more claims of destroyed or damaged trucks than ever before, but photo confirmation of the claims continued to be unsatisfactory. Because the photo interpreters wanted to use the large format KA-1 photographs in their search for the destroyed trucks, in February 1970 the 460th Tactical Reconnaissance Wing designated the RF-101C the primary reconnaissance aircraft for BDA missions in Commando Hunt III. Flying low over the roads and waterways of the Ho Chi Minh Trail, the Voodoos brought back clear, sharp, big photographs and there was some increase in the number of claims verified by aerial photography. [40]

North Vietnamese Trucks heading South. Finding and destroying these trucks was hard enough, confirming reports of truck kills was even harder.

Source: Vietnamese People's Liberation Army

Commando Hunt III also tested proposed new procedures for monitoring enemy truck movements and road repair. RF-101C and RF-4C pilots orbited their aircraft at specified points until the Airborne Battlefield Command and Control Center (ABCCC) called upon them to photograph some target that fighters had bombed or strafed. The RF-101C pilots photographed the scene before the North Vietnamese could remove or conceal the strike evidence, and their film received priority processing so the Seventh Air Force commander could evaluate the results in a minimum of time. Reconnaissance pilots also photographed designated road sectors at first light, hoping to record truck kills before the North Vietnamese could remove the hulks. [41]

Much of the Commando Hunt area and North Vietnam experienced exceptionally poor weather during the final weeks of 1969 and the first few weeks of 1970, restricting the RF-101C's to missions over South Vietnam. whenever the weather broke over North Vietnam, the pilots flew every available reconnaissance aircraft to satisfy urgent intelligence needs. when the weather was bad in the north, Seventh Air Force headquarters scheduled sorties against only the higher priority objectives, releasing reconnaissance aircraft for use in western Laos or South Vietnam. [42]

On many of the missions in South Vietnam, the pilots photographed top priority objectives such as troops in contact, convoy ambushes, and hostile troop movements. In such cases, Seventh Air Force headquarters either diverted an airborne reconnaissance aircraft or scrambled the RF-101C in alert status. Although it was effective, Seventh Air Force did away with the RF-101C alert on 19 April 1970 as an economy measure. Instead, one crew always was on call for high priority scramble missions, and the maintenance crews had to keep one RF-101C available. Scramble time under such changed conditions was much longer, but the new procedure saved many aircraft hours that could be used to good advantage in other ways. [43]

With the departure from SEA of a squadron of RF-4Cs, Seventh Air Force headquarters increased the RF-101C sortie rate to 1.0 per aircraft per day. The Voodoos often had exceeded that rate without difficulty, so it was not an unreasonable requirement. RF-101C pilots continued to fly most of the reconnaissance sorties over North Vietnam south of $17^0 15'$ N., usually without escort. Even in that relatively lightly defended area, however, the potential threat increased significantly. Mobile SAM battalions roamed the panhandle roads, setting up and launching within a very short time. MiG-21s, a very serious threat because of their superior speed and modern armament, patrolled the panhandle as far south as Dong Hoi. Seventh Air Force headquarters in March 1970 reluctantly agreed that the RF-101C pilots could fly reconnaissance sorties over North Vietnam at 400 to 500 feet AGL, which would foil the SAMs and reduce the threat from the MiGs. The North Vietnamese promptly increased their concentrations of automatic weapons along the roads and around key objectives, causing Seventh Air Force headquarters to raise the minimum altitude to 4,500 feet over North Vietnam. By the end of March 1970, SAM sites protected the Mu Gia and Ban Karai Passes and Route 7.[44]

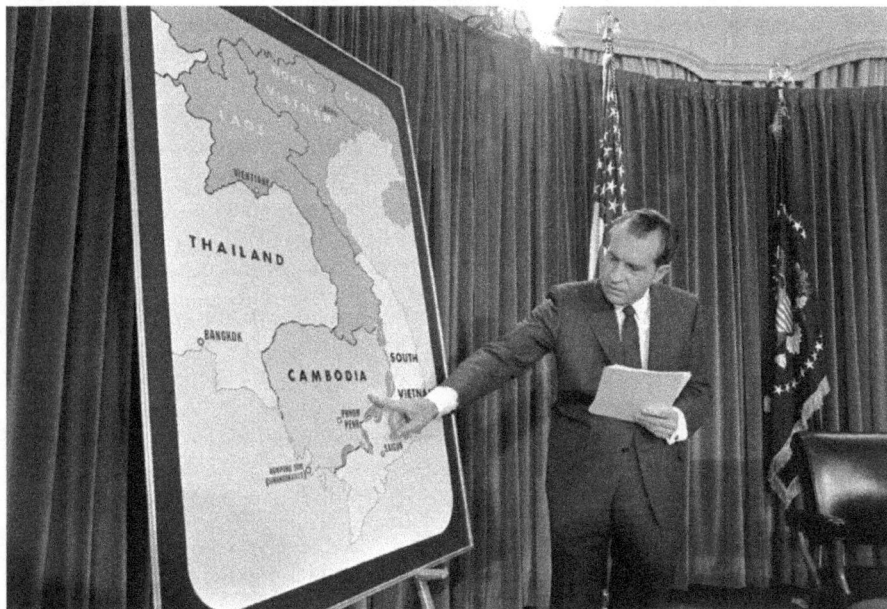

President Nixon explains operations in Cambodia. Source: U.S. Air Force

President Richard M. Nixon on 30 April 1970 announced that he had ordered attacks "to clean out major enemy sanctuaries on the Cambodia-Vietnam border." He tied the move to his withdrawal of 150,000 troops from SEA and promised that all US. forces would leave Cambodia by 30 June. On 6 May, the JCS authorized tactical reconnaissance over Cambodia to a depth of 60 nautical miles, but directed that the aircraft not fly over Phnom Penh. Earlier RF-101C missions over Cambodia, limited in scope and number, had operated under the nickname French Leave, but at the end of May, CINCPAC assigned the nickname Face

Value to all photo reconnaissance activities in Cambodia and directed that no other nickname be used. Face Value missions covered entirely new territory, causing the pilots to photograph such potential targets as roads, waterways, cities, military bases, airfields, and industrial complexes.[45]

Photography and visual reconnaissance showed that the Khmer Rouge insurgents and North Vietnamese were using the Se Kong and Tonle Kong Rivers between Attopeu and Strung Treng to move cargo and troops toward Phnom Penh and other large cities. CINCPAC approved continuous reconnaissance over the rivers and other key transportation routes to maintain a current order of battle. The JCS gradually enlarged the reconnaissance operations area to include all of Cambodia, although in some areas specific approval was required for each mission. The RF-101Cs remained active over Cambodia because their large format photographs continued to be favored by Air Force photo interpreters and ground unit commands.[46]

Supplies captured in the effort to eliminate sanctuaries. Source: U.S. Air Force

Reconnaissance sorties over Cambodia more than doubled during June 1970 as Seventh Air Force diverted many of the sorties formerly allocated to South Vietnam. Seventh Air Force used the RF-101Cs and RF-4Cs from Tan Son Nhut Air Base for most of the Cambodia sorties, leaving the RF-4Cs at Udorn RTAFB to handle the sorties over Laos and North Vietnam. The RF-101C pilots, however, also continued their unescorted sorties over North Vietnam just above the DMZ. As the weather in Laos deteriorated in July and the enemy activity along those infiltration routes ground to a halt, the RF-101C pilots flew no missions over Laos for many weeks.[48]

In February 1970, the Air Force Chief of Staff proposed withdrawing the RF-101Cs of the 45th Tactical Reconnaissance Squadron from SEA. He wanted to inactivate the only remaining RF-101C squadron, which in turn would allow him to phase out a training unit with 16 RF-101Cs, saving a considerable amount of money each year. Even though the KA-1 large format camera was the only satisfactory medium altitude camera in SEA, its withdrawal would not cripple the reconnaissance effort. Despite the unpopularity of its small format cameras and its lack of a medium altitude capability, the RF-4C could accomplish much of the work that the RF-101Cs had been doing. Seventh Air Force headquarters and MACV at first opposed the withdrawal because of the high value which they placed on the KA-1 photography, but in time they reluctantly agreed that the budgetary restrictions imposed by the Congress left no other alternative.

Detachment 1, 45th Tactical Reconnaissance Squadron, halted all reconnaissance operations on 1 November 1970 and prepared to disband. Air Force headquarters had ordered that the squadron transfer the RF-101Cs to Meridian, Mississippi, where they would replace the RF-84Fs in an Air National Guard reconnaissance squadron. The last RF-101C left Tan Son Nhut Air Base on 16 November on its long journey to its stateside home, and on that date PACAF inactivated Detachment 1 of the 45th Tactical Reconnaissance Squadron.

The Voodoo, among the first U.S. tactical jet aircraft involved in the SEA conflict, went home before the fighting ended. Combat action had destroyed 35 RF-101Cs, almost the equivalent of the maximum authorized strength (i.e., 36 aircraft) of the two reconnaissance wings stationed in SEA. Actually, the total of RF-101Cs in SEA, from August 1966 to January 1967, never reached more than 32. But, the Voodoo served long and well, and contributed substantially to whatever success the U.S. and allied forces had achieved.[49]

CHAPTER V .. AFTERMATH
By Defense Lion Publications

There can be little doubt that the RF-101C force was gravely damaged by the war in Vietnam. A total of 35 RF-101C aircraft had been lost, 21 percent of the total production run of 166. Of these, 1 was shot down by a MiG-21, 1 was destroyed on the ground by artillery fire, 5 are known or believed to have been brought down by SAMs, 6 were lost to mechanical failure or other accidents, and 22 were shot down by automatic weapons fire, usually from radar-guided 37mm and 57mm guns. Yet, this wasn't the primary problem. By the time the aircraft returned to the States, their performance was much worse than the official documentation suggested. The aircraft's drag had been increased by the skin patches and plates applied to repair battle damage or remedy wear and tear. This also increased the weight of the aircraft. Also, the maintenance problems with the J-57 engines resulted in their power output being cut back to preserve what was left of engine life. As a result, the RF-101Cs returning from Southeast Asia had their tactical radius reduced by nearly 30 percent, their ferry range cut by more than 40 percent, and their service ceiling reduced by 15 percent. Hard service had demonstrably worn the aircraft out. They were quickly retired from the frontline Air Force and assigned to the Air National Guard.

Yet, the Vietnam War had also highlighted the virtues of the RF-101C. Its long range and high performance enabled it to provide wide-ranging coverage, while its flexible camera equipment produced images of unsurpassed quality. The product of its reconnaissance missions was considered much better and more useful than that of the RF-4C. The low-level missions carried out by the RF-101Cs allowed them to photograph targets that were hidden under tree cover in ways that high-flying reconnaissance aircraft and satellites could not. By the time the RF-101Cs returned from Southeast Asia, it was already recognized that the U.S. reconnaissance force was seriously under-strength and needed immediate reinforcement.

Part of the solution had already been found by exploiting TAC's force of F-101A and F-101C fighter-bombers. They were surplus to TAC requirements yet had flown relatively few hours. They were therefore earmarked for conversion to reconnaissance aircraft. In 1965, work had started on converting 29 F-101As. The armament and radar were removed and replaced by a new nose housing a pallet of side- and forward-facing cameras. These aircraft were redesignated RF-101G and could be distinguished from the RF-101A by their shorter and broader nose. The RF-101Gs were assigned to the Air National Guard. They were followed by 31 RF-101Hs that had been obtained by conversion of F-101Cs. These aircraft would supplement the surviving RF-101Cs for a decade, with the last being withdrawn by the end of 1979.

A further effort to reinforce the RF-101 fleet was less successful. A total of 22 Canadian CF-101B interceptors had been returned to the United States following their replacement by updated F-101Bs. They were modified as two-seat reconnaissance aircraft, with the armament and fire control system replaced by a battery of three KS-87B cameras in forward, left split vertical, and right split vertical configurations, plus two AXQ-2 television cameras in forward-looking and downward-looking positions. The pilot's cockpit was equipped with a TV viewfinder control indicator. These modified aircraft were redesignated RF-101B and entered service in late 1971. The hope had been that they would at least partially compensate for the aircraft lost over Southeast Asia, but the aircraft turned out to be extremely expensive to operate and systems problems required major time and funding investments in order to maintain operating standards. The RF-101Bs were phased out of service by 1972.

With the RF-101s gone, the U.S. tactical reconnaissance fleet standardized on the RF-4C. This aircraft also had an impressive record, having flown day missions until 1972 over North and South Vietnam as well as Laos. No RF-4Cs were lost to MiGs, but seven were shot down by SAMs and 65 were destroyed by AAA or small arms fire. Four were destroyed on the ground and seven were lost in operational accidents. However, considering the total number of missions flown, the loss rate was relatively low. During the 1980s, the RF-4C fleet was progressively modernized, but the numbers available shrank steadily. The type saw its last operational service during Operation Desert Storm, flying over Kuwait almost every day in search of Republican Guard units. They also searched for rocket fuel plants, chemical weapons plants, and command and communications centers. As Iraqi Scud attacks proliferated, the RF-4Cs were used to hunt the Scud launchers hiding in western Iraq. Once Operation Desert Storm was over, the last RF-4Cs were withdrawn from service.

Very early in the F-15 Eagle program, McDonnell Douglas had proposed an RF-15 that would have been equipped with a new nose containing cameras, side-looking airborne radar, television cameras, and a multispectral scanner. This proposal was rejected by the Air Force, and no dedicated reconnaissance version of the Eagle was ever built. In addition, an RF-16 reconnaissance aircraft was proposed by Lockheed Martin in response to a 1988 USAF requirement to replace the RF-4Cs. These aircraft would have carried the ATARS (Advanced Tactical Air Reconnaissance System) centerline pod. This had a flexible mix of sensors, including an electro-optical videotape system that allows images to be transmitted via digital datalink to a ground station, providing ground commanders with reconnaissance capabilities in real time. The proposal was not successful, and with it, the dedicated tactical reconnaissance fighter appears to have disappeared from Air Force thinking. The role has been largely taken over by remotely piloted aircraft.

NOTES FOR CHAPTER I

1. Hist (S/XGDS), AMC, Jul-Dec 56, III, Pt. a, p. 87.

2. Ibid., pp. 87-88.

3. Ibid., Chronology.

4. Ibid., p. 89.

5. Ibid., pp. 239, 240.

6. Ibid., pp. 90, 236.

7. Ibid., pp. 90-91.

8. Ibid., pp. 236-240.

9. Ibid., pp. 91, 230, 236, 237.

10. Ibid., pp. 100, 237.

11. Weapons System Summary (S/NOF0RN/AFEO), USAF, Dir of Management Analysis, 12 Feb 59.

12. Monograph (U), AFLC, The RF-101 Voodoo at Ogden Air Materiel Area, Aug 52-Jun 62, p. 159.

13. Ibid., p. 161; pub (S), PACAF Planning Factors, RF-l0lC, PFCAG 3168, 1 Mar 58.

14. Pub (S), PACAF Planning Factors, RF-l0lC, PFCAG 3168, Mar 58, p. 5.

15. Monograph (U), AFLC, The RF-l0l Voodoo at Ogden Air Materiel Area, Aug 52-Jun 62, p. 155.

16. Pub (S), PACAF Planning Factors, RF-l0lC, PFCAG 3168, I Mar 58, p. 14.

17. Rprt (S/XGDS), APGC, Final Report on Employment and Suitability Test of RF-l0l Day Reconnaissance Aircraft Project No. APG/TAT/399-A pp 4, 5-6, 11, 15-16, 35

18. Ibid, pp. 19-20; AFM 55-6, Tactical Air Reconnaissance, 24 Sep 70.

19. Rprt (U), Final Report on employment and Suitability Test of the KA-2 Camera, Hq. APGC Proj No. APG/CSC/434-A, 15 Jan 57.

20, Rprt (U), Final Report on Employment and Suitability Test of the KA-1 Camera, Hq. APGC Proj No. APG/533-A, 10 Jan 57.

21. AFM 55-6, Tactical Air Reconnaissance, 24 Sep 70.

22.   Rprt (s), APGC Final Report on Employment and Suitability Test of the RF-101A Day Reconnaissance Aircraft, APGC Project No. APG/TAT/399-A

NOTES FOR CHAPTER II

1.   Rprt (U), Project CORONA HARVEST Physical and Cultural Environment of Southeast Asia, 1 Nov 68.

2.   Msg (S), AAIRA to CSAF, lnfo State, PACAF, et al Vientiane CX-A-9 to SECSTATE, 271432Z Dec 60; hist (TS), PACAF, Jul-Dec 61, I, Pt. 2, p. 16.

3.   Hist (TS), PACAF, Jan-Jun 61, III Pt. 1, A-2, Feb, p. 1

4.   Msg (S), SECSTATE 1067 to AMEMBASSY Vientiane, 3 Apr 61 ; msg (Ss), AMEMBASSYVientiane 1814 to SECSTATE, 4 Apr 61; msg (S) 13AF to 13AF ADVON et al, 13ODC/1/01238A, Apr 61; rprt (S) Project CORONA HARVEST Special-Report No. 70-11, Able Mable, Jan 70, p.2; Capt. Mark E. Smith, USAF Reconnaissance in Southeast Asia, !991-1966 (TS/NOFORN)(HQ PACAF, project CHECO, 25 Oct 66). p. 1; hist (S) 18th Tac Ftr Wg, Jan-Jun 61, p. 74; hist (TS) PACAF, Jul-Dec 61, I, Pt. 2, p. 17; hist (S), 5AF, Jan-Jun 61, I, p.124.

5.   Msg (U), 13 ODM 05419, Mobile Yoke Frag Order No. 2 undated; hist (S), 13AF, Jan-Jun 60, I, pp. 36-37.

6.   Hist (S) PACAF Jan-Jun 61, I, p. 96; hist (S) 5AF Jan-Jun 61, I, p. 98.

7.   Rprt (S), Project CORONA HARVEST Special Report No 70-11' Able Mable, Jan 70, P. 2

8.   Smith USAF Reconnaissance in Southeast Asia. 1961-1966 p. 2.

9,   Ibid; hist (S) 2d ADVON, 15 Nov 61-8 Oct 62 II; rprt (S), Project CORONA HARVEST special Report No. 70-11, Able Mable Jan 70, p. 3.

10.   Hist (TS), PACAF, Jul-Dec 61, III, Pt. 1, A-2, Oct, p 3.

11.   Msg (C), 13AF to PACAF et al, 13 ODC 1-0352A, O40935Z Nov 61; rprt (TS), Fifth Air Force in the Southeast Asia Crisis, 30 Jan 52, Hq. 5AF.

12.   Msg (C), CINCPAC to JCS, 110011Z Nov 61; msg (C) 13AF to 13 ADVON et al, 13 ODC 1-0336A, 050538Z Nov 61; msg (C), 13 ADVON to 13AF, ADVON A.M. 11-109, 080245Z Nov 61; hist (S), 13AF Jul-Dec t1, pp. 69,98; rprt (S), Project CORONA HARVEST Special Report No. 70-11, Able Mable, Jan 70, p. 4; ltr (S), Det 10, 2d ADVON, undated, subj: report on Activities Under PACAF OPSorder 220-62 (ABLE MABLE) to 1 March 1962.

13. Rprt (S), Project CORONA HARVEST Special Report No. 70-11 Able Mable, Jan 70, pp. 8-13.

L4. Msg (S), CHMAAG Laos to 13AF ADVON, ML-EVAL 5368, 0606452 Nov 61; msg (S), CINCPAC to CITMAAG Laos, 1001202 Nov 61; msg.(S), CINCPAC Laos to 13AF, ML-EVAL 5474, 100450Z Nov 61.

15. Msg (S), PACAF to 13AF, PFCVC 556, 30 Nov 61.

16. Hist (S), 2d ADVoN, 15 Nov 61-8 Oct 62, I, p. 6; Sec Def Book (TS), for January Meeting, 16 Dec 61.

17. Hist (S), 13AF, Jul-Dec 61, I, pp. 69-70, and 1962, I, p. II-62; hist (TS), PACAF, Jul-Dec 61, .III, pt. l, A-2 Dec, p. 3.

18. Hist (TS), PACAF, Jan-Jun 62, III, Pt. 1, A-2

19. Msg (C), 13AF to PACAF, 13 ODO-R/COC/02-069, 1715OZ Feb 62.

20. Msg (C), 13AF to 2d ADVON, 130DC 2-057A, 20095OZ Feb 62.

21. Ltr (S), Det. 1.0, 2d ADVON, undated, subj: Report on Activities Under PACAF OPSorder 220-62 (ABLE MABLE) to 1 March 1962; Sec Def Book (TS) for March Meeting, 1962.

22, Msg (C), 13AF, to PACAF, 13 IDC-2/0362A, 140747Z May 62: ltr (S), 13AF to 2d ADVON, subj: Major and Incipient Problem Areas at Detachment 10, APO 74, Box 311, 14 Mar 62; Ltr (S)., 20DC to 2 DAS, subj: Problem Areas at Det 10, 2d ADVON, 22 Mar 62; Memo (S), 2d ADVON, 2 IDC to 2 DAS, subj: Problem Areas at Det. 10, 25 Mar 62.

23. Msg (C), 5AF to PACAF, 5 FOOT-O-T 0360C, 270735Z Mar 62; msg (C), 13AF to PACAF, 13 ODO-R/2/1316A, 051000Z Apr 62; ltr (C), Det 10, 2d ADVON, undated, subj: Report on Activities under PACAF OPSorder 220-62 (ABLE MABLE) to 1 March 1962.

24. Hist (S), 39th Air Div, Jul 61 - Jun 62, pp. l0-12.

25. Rprt (U), TAC rprt TR-63-15, Operational Test and Evaluation, RF-101 "Toy Tiger" Configuration, Aug 63.

26. Book (TS), Sec Def Book for March Meeting, 1962.

27. Rprt (U), TAC rprt TR-63-15, Operational Test and Evaluation, RF-101 "Toy Tiger" Configuration, Aug 63.

28. Msg (C) 13AF to JTF-116, 13 OOT-W/2/1636A, msg 423 141230A Jul 62; msg (C), 5AF to 18 Tac Ftr Wg et al, 5 FOOT-0-T 050T, 080537Z Jun 62; msg (C), PACAF to 13AF et al, PFODC-OCO 1362-62, 30 Aug 62; msg (S), 2AD to PACAF, 2 ODC-R-62-0003L 021030Z Jun 63.

29. Rprt (U), TAC rprt TR-63-15, Operational Test and Evaluation, RF-101 "ToyTiger" Configuration, Aug 63.

30.   Msg (C), 13AF to PACAF, 13 CCR 06046, 091111Z Jun 62; msg (C), 13AF to PACAF, 13 ODC-2-199A, 010652Z Jun 62; msg (C), 13AF to AFCC JTF 116, 13 OOT-W/2/l1598A, #332, 300432Z Jun 62; msg (S), 13AF to PACAF, 13 PPT/2/1637A, 141230Z2 Jul 62; msg (C), 13AF to PACAF, 13 ODC 2-3144.

31.   Msg (C), 13AF to PACAF, 13 OOT 2/1716A, 140945Z Aug 62; msg (C), 13AF to 6010 Tac Gp et al, 13 OOT/2/1723A, 170840Z Aug 62; msg (C), CINCPAC to PACAF, 151858Z Aug 62; Project CORONA HARVEST Special Report No. 70-11, Able Mable, Jan 70, P. 21.

32.   Msg (C), PACAF to 13AF, PFOCO 62-1834J, 2 Sep 62.

33.   Msg (S), PACAF to 2d ADVON, 13 IDC, 18-9-35, 181200Z Sep 62.

34.   Msg (C), PACAF to 13AF, 6010 Tac Gp, PFOCO-S-62-1120; msg (S), CINCPAC to PACAF, 292115Z Sep 67; msg (C), PACAF to 13AF, 6010 Tac Gp, PFOCO-S-62-1202, 6 Nov 62; msg (S), 6010 Tac Gp to PACAF, RTF 244, 08152OZ Nov 62.

35.   Msg (C), CINCPAC 102204Z Nov 62; msg (C) 2AD to 6010 Tac Gp, 2 ODC-R-62-2081K, 130712Z; msg (S) CINCPAC to JCS 062112Z Oct 62.

36.   Hist (S), 5AF, Jul-Dec 62'T; hist (S), 39th Air Div, Jul-Dec 62, I, pp. 63-64; msg (C), 13AF to PACAF 13 TPC-2-402A, 150211Z Nov 62; msg (C) PACAF to 13AF, PFCDC 1-1815-62, 26 Nov 62; msg (C), CINCPAC to PACAF, 261935Z Nov 62; hist (S) 2AD Jan-Jun 64, I, pp. 110-111; msg (C), 2AD to PACAF, 2 ODC-R-62-2215K, 050340Z Dec 62; rprt (S), Project CORONA HARVEST Special Report No 70-11 (ABLE MABLE), Jan 70, p. 21.

37.   Hist (S), 18 TFW, Jan-Jun 63, I, P. 76: Tab 10 to Memo (TS), ACS/Plans-to DCS/P&O, Hq. PACAF, 14 Nov 62.

38.   Msg (C), I3AF to PACAF, 13 CCR-156A, 05024lZ Dec 62.

(large section of text missing from the original document)

63.   Hist (C), 313th Air Div, Jul 64 - Jun 65, I, pp. 302-303; hist (TS/NOFORN), PACAF, Jan - Jun 64, I, Pt. 2, p. L29: MacNaughton, Yankee Team, May 64 - Jan 65, p. 18.

64.   Study (S), TARC, 21 May 65, A Review and Analysis of Tactical Air Reconnaissance Programs in Southeast Asia, Jan 62 - May 65, p. 286; hist (S/NOFORN), 2AD, Jan - Jun 64, I, pp. 112-113.

65.   Hist (S/NOFORN/AFEO), TAC, Jul-Dec 64, p. 557; hist (C), 313th Air Div, Jul 64-Jun 65, I, p. 302; study (TS/NOFORN), 5AF, 5AF Reactions to the Tonkin Gulf Crisis, 4-15 August 1964.

56.   Report on the War in Vietnam (U), CINCPAC and COMUSMACV Washington: GPO, 1968, p. 13.

67. Hist (TS/NOFORN), PACAF, Jan-Jun 64, I, Pt. 2, p. 140; hist (S/NOFORN), 13AF, Jan-Dec 64, I, p. II-49; MacNaughton, Yankee Team, May 64-Jun Q, p. 18.

68. Proposed ltr (S), 2AD, subj: New Yankee Team Concept, 20 Aug 64.

69. Ltr (S), MACV to CINCPAC, subj: Reconnaissance North of 20 Degrees in Laos, serial 00591, 16 Dec 64.

70. Hist (S), 5AF, Jan-Dec 64, I, p. 73; hist (S), 18th Tac Ftr Wg, Jul-Dec 64, I, pp. 47-48; msg (S), 80th TFSq to 2AD, 80 TFS KOCYT-944-64.

71. Msg (S), COMUSMACV to CINCPAC, MACJ-31 14789, 240350Z Nov 65.

72. Msg (S), Det. 2, 18 TFW to 2AD, Det 2 18 TFW 00053 Jan 65, 170815Z.

73. Hist (S/NOFORN), 2AD, Jul-Dec 64, V, Doc 38.

NOTES FOR CHAPTER III

1. Msg (S), 18th Tac Ftr Wg to 13AF and 2AD, 18 DCOT-00475 Jan 65, 050650Z Jan 65; msg (S), l8th Tac Ftr Wg to 13AF and 2AD, 18 DCO 00465. Jan 65, 300400Z Jan 65; MacNaughton, Yankee Team, May 64 - Jun 65, p. 36.

2. Rprt (U), TAC, Operational Test and Evaluation of Modification 1181/RF-101, Apr 65; hist (S/NOFORN), 39th Air Div, Jan-Jun 65, pp. 25-26.

3. Hist (C), 313th Air Div, Jul 64-Jun 65, I, pp. 309-310; MacNaughton, Yankee Team, May 64- Jun 65, p. 35; msg (S), CINCPACAF to 5AF, VC 00082, 200019Z Jan 64.

4. Msg (s), 13AF to CINCPACAF, 13 ODX 90058 Apr 65, 050050Z Apr 65; rprt (S), end-of-tour, Lt. Col. Robert P. Coombs, Recce Staff Off, 2AD, undated; MACV Monthly Evaluation Report (S/NOFORN), Feb 65, p. 21.

5. Tab C, Flaming Dart (S).

6. Msg (C), CINCPACAF to CINCPAC, DOCOS 00085 Feb 65.

7. Msg (S/NOFORN), 2AD, 2OPR-65-TS-1679 Feb 65.

8. Analysis of Air Operations, Southeast Asia (S), AFXOPLC, 5 Apr 65, pp. 4-3, 4-4; rprt (U), Report on the War in Vietnam, CINCPAC and COMUSMACV, Washington: GPO, 1968, p. 16.

9. Hist (TS/NOFORN), PACAF, Jul 64-Jun 65, III, pE. 2, pp. 114-115.

10.	Msg (TS), CINCPACAF to 5AF, I3AF, and 2AD, DO 30107 Apr 65, 150201Z; hist (TS/NOFORN), PACAF, Jul 64-Jun 65, I, pr. 1, p. 21, and II, Pt. 2, hist of DOPL, Apr 65.

11.	Hist (S), PACAF, Jul 64-Jun 65, III, Pt. 2, Opens; hist (S/NOFORN), 15AF, Jan-Dec 65, I, pp. 43-44; hist (C), 313th Air Div, Jul 64-Jun 65, pp. 309-316; hist (S/NOFORN), 39th Air Div, Jan-Jun 65, p. 24.

12.	Hist (TS), PACAF, Jul 64-Jun 65, III, Pt. 2, Opens.

13.	Rprt (S), CINC US Pacific Fleet, The United States Navy in the Pacific, 1965 p. 206; PACAF Pub (S/NOFORN), Effects of Air Operations in Southeast Asia, 19 Aug 65, p. 5.

14.	Hist (TS/NOFRN), PACAF, Jul 64-Jun 65, II, pt. 2, Recce Div Hist; hist (TS/NOFORN/AFEO), PACAF, Jul 64 - Dec 65, II, Pt. 23 msg (TS), CINCPAC to CINCPACFLT and CINCPACAF, 1704512 Nov 65; msg (TS), 2AD to CINCPACAF, Doco-E-65-Ts-24586 Nov 65, 210140Z; PACAF Pub (S), Effects of Air Operations in Southeast Asia, 30 Sep 66, p. 13.

15.	Hist (S), 15 TRS, Jul - Dec 65, p. 62.

16.	Hist (S), 313th Air Div, Jul 64 - Jun 65, I, p. 312.

17.	Hist (S), 363d TRW, Jul-Dec 65, p. 13; TAC M.O. 13, 9 Oct 65; hist (S),6250th CSGp, Jul-Dec 65, p. 19; hist (C), 20th TRSq, 13 Nov-31 Dec 65, p. l; PACAF S.O. G-186, 2 Nov 65; hist (TS), Recce Div, Dir of plans & Req, Dep for Opns, 2AD, Jul-Dec 65.

18.	Hist (S), 16th TRS, Jan-Jun 66; msg (S), CINCPACAF to 13AF, 140053Z Dec 65, 54543; msg (S), 13AF to CINCPACAF, L602S7Z Dec 65, 28672; ltr (S), AFXOPFR to AFXDC, 12 Aug 66, subj: 460th Tactical Reconnaissance Wing (SEA) PACAF Summary Air Operations SEA (TS), XV|II, 4-17 Feb 66, pp. 6-1 to 6-2; PACAF S.O. G-41, 15 Feb 66; PACAF S.O. G-51, 25 Feb 66; hist (TS), PAC,A,F, Jan-Dec 65, I, Pt. 1, p. 8.

19.	Hist (S/Gp-4), 15 TRS, Jan-Dec 66, pp. 14-15; hist (S), 20th TRS, Jan-Jun 66, p. l; hist (S/NOFORN/AFEO), 7AF, Jan 66-Jun 67, I, p. xvii; PACAF S.O. c-94, 30 Mar 66; hist (S), 377th CSGp, Jan-Jun 66, Supp. Doc; PACAF M.O. #10, 27 Jun 66; hist (S), Recce Div, Dir Plans & Req, 7AF, Jan-Jun 66.

20.	Hist (S), 20th IRs, Jan-Jun 66; hist (S/NOFORN), 5AF, Jan-Jun 66, II, p. 206; hist (S), Recce Div, Dlr plans & Req, 7AF, Jan-Jun 66.

21.	Ltr (U), 2AD DITM to DO, 1g Dec 65.

22.	Hist (S), 15th TRS, Jul-Dec 65, pp. 1o-11.

23. Rprt (U), Report on the War in Vietnam , CINCPAC and COMUSMACV, Washington: GPO, 1968, p. 23; hist (S), 15th TRS, Jan-Dec 66, pp. 1-8.

24. Hist (S), 15th TRS, Jan-Dec 66, pp. 5-6.

25. Ibid, p. 8.

26. Ibid, p. 9; PACAF Summary (TS/NOFORN/AFEO), Air Operations, Southeast Asia, XIV, 24 Dec-6 Jan 66, p. 2-1.

27. Hist (S), 15th TRS, Jan - Jun 65, p. 14.

28. Hist (S), 15th TRS, Jul - Dec 65, p. 62.

29. Ibid, pp. 8-9.

30. PACAF pub (S/NOFORN), Effects of Air operations in Southeast Asia, 25 Nov 65, p. 8; 2AD Weekly Air Intel Summary (S/NOFORN), I, No. l, 19 Nov 65, p. 11.

31. PACAF pub (S/NOFRN), Effects of Air Operations, Southeast Asia, 9 Dec 65, pp. 4-5.

32. 7AF WAIS (S/NOFCRN), III, No. 2, 9 Jan 67, p. 8.

33. PACAF summary (TS/NOFORN/AFEO), Air operations, Southeast Asia, XVI, 21-Jan - 3 Feb 66.

34. Hist (S), 15th TS, Jan-Mar 67, p. 1l; hist (S), 45th TRS, Jul-Dec 66, p. 6.

35. Hist (S/Gp-4), 15th TRS, Jan - Dec 66, pp. 10-11; hist 45th TRS, Jan-Jun 66, pp. 3-4

36. Hist (C), 45th TRS, Jan-Mar 67, pp. 3-4; PACAF Summery (TS/AFEO) Air Ops SEA, XXXI, Feb 67, p. 4 – 15; Lee Bonetti, The War In Vietnam, Jan – Jun 67 (S/NOFORN(HQ PACAF Project CHECO, 29 April 86) pp. 43 – 44; PACAF Summary (TS/NOFORN/AFEO), Air Ops SEA, XXXIII, p.7-B-2

37. Hist (S/Gp-4), 15th TRS, Jan-Dec 66, p. 58.

38. Hist (S/Gp-4), 15th TRS, Jan-Dec 66, App. 3, p. 86; hist (U) 20th TRS, Jan – Jun 66 p. 5; msg (S) 7602 AINTELG to AFSHRC, #4685, 211745Z Jun 78

39. PACAF Summary (TS/NOFORN/AFEO), Air Ops SEA, XXII, l May 66, p. 4-4

40. Hist (S/Gp-4), 15th TRS, Jan-Dec 66, p. 11; PACAF summary (TS/NOFORN), Air Ops SEA, XXXVIII, Sep 67, p. 5 – 9

41. Hist (S), 15th TRS, Jan-Mar 67, p. 11; hist (S), 45th TRS, Jul-Dec 66, p. 6.

42. Hist (S/Gp-4), 15th TRS, Jan-Dec 66, App. 3, p. 86; hist (U), 20th TRS, Jan-Jun 66, p. 5.

43.   Msg (S), 7AF to CINCPAC, DO/DI-66-TS-12669, Jul 66; msg (S), 7AF to PACAF, C-66-TS-14991 Aug 66; msg (S), 7AF to PACAF VC-145 Jul 66, 171145Z; msg (S), CINCPAC to CINCPACFLT et al, 2604122 Aug 66; msg (S), PACAF to 7AF, Fastel D0 07l, 18225Z Sep 66.

44.   Msg (S), CINCPACAF to 7AF, DO 31415 Sep 66, 270420Z Sep 65.

45.   PACAF Summary (TS/NOFORN/AFEO), Air Ops SEA, XVI, 21 Jan-3 Feb 66, p. 2-10.

46.   Ltr (TS/AFEO), 7AF, DOA-CHECO, subj: Historical Documents, 12 Jul 67; hist (TS/NOFORN), PACAF, Jan-Dec 67, I, Pt. 2, pp. 430-431; hist (S/NOFORN), 7AF, DCS/Intelligence, Jul-Dec 66, p. 13.

47.   Hist (S), Recce Div, Dir Plans & Req, 7AF, Jan-Jun 66; PACAF Summary (TS/NOFORN/AFEO), Air Ops SEA, XXV, Aug 66, p.4-l; PACAF S.0. G-269, 8 Sep 66; Warren A. Trest, TSGT Charles E. Garland, SSGT Dale E. Harmons, USAF Posture in Thailand, 1966 (SECRET/NOFORN)(HQ PACAF, Project CHECO, 28 Aug 67). II Doc 15.

48.   Msg (S), 7AF to CINCPACAF, Do-66-TS-21678 Dec 66.

49.   Hist (S), 460th TRW, Jan-Mar 67, Hist of DC/I; rprt (S/AFEO), Oral History Discussion by Col Adrian M. Burrows, Lt. Col. Thomas Killion, and Major Daniel E. Freeland, 1 Dec 69; personal experience of author.

50.   Hist (C), 45th TRS, Jan-Mar 67, pp. 3-4; PACAF Summary (TS/AFEO), Air Ops SEA, XXXI, Feb 67, p.4-15; Lee Bonetti, The War In Vietnam, Jan -Jun 67, pp. 43-44; PACAF Summary (TS/NOFORN/AFEO), Air Ops SEA, XXXIII , p. 7-B-2.

51.   Msg (S), 7AF to CINCPACAF, C-02298 Feb 67, 1109052: 7AF WAIS (S/NOFORN), 67-9, 19 Feb 67, p. 18, and 67-10, 5 Mar 67, p.4; PACAF Summary (TS/AFEO), Air Ops SEA, XXXI, Feb 67, pp. 4-3 to 4-11; USAF Daily Summary (U), 7AF Dir of Information, 11 Feb 67, Bonetti, The Air War in Vietnam, Jan-Jun 67, p. 44.

52.   Hist (S), 460th TRW, Jan-Mar 67, hist of 12th TRS, p. 8, and hist of DC/I, pp. 3-4.

53.   Hist (S), 355th TFW, Jan-Jun 67, I, p. 5.

54.   Ibid. p. 14; hist (S), 432d TRW, Jan-Jun 67, II, hist of 20th TRS; 7AF WAIS (S/NOFORN), 67-23, 4 Jun 67, p.2.

NOTES FOR CHAPTER IV

1.   Hist (S), 45th TRS, Apr-Jun 67, p. 5; PACAF Summary (TS/NOTORN/AFEO), Air Ops SEA, XXXVI, Jul 67, p. 4-3.

2.   Hist (C),460th TRW, Jul-Sep 67, Hist of Det. 1, 45th TRS.

3.   Hist (S), 460th TRW, Apr-Jun 68, p. 29.

4.   Ltr (C), General John D. Ryan to General Momyer, 26 Jun 67; 7AF WAIS (S/OFORN), 67-27, 2 Jul 67, p. 36.

5.   Hist (S), 7AF, Jul-Dec 67, I, p. 33; hist (TS/NOFORN/AFEO), PACAF, 1967, I, Pt. 2, p. 374; PACAF Summary (TS/NOFORN/AFEO), Air Ops SEA, XXXVII, Aug 67; Lee Bonetti, Maj. A. W. Thompson, Melvin F. Porter, C. William Thorndale, The War in Vietnam, Jul-Dec 67 (S/NOFORN) (HQ PACAF, Project CHECO, 29 Nov 68), p. 33.

6.   Hist (C), 460th TRW, Apr-Jun 67, Hist of DCO; hist (S),460th TRW, Jul- Sep 67, Hist of DCS Operations, par. 6, and hist of DCS Materiel, p, 1; hist (C), 12th RITS, Jul 65-Jun 70, p.2.

7.   Hist (C), 460th TRW, Jul-Sep 67, Hist of DCS/M and hist of DCO, and hist of Det. 1, 45th TRS; hist (S), 460th TRW, Oct-Dec 67, Hist of DC/M, p. 1; PACAF Summary (TS/NOFORN/AFEO), Air Ops SEA, XLI, Dec 67, p. 4-24; rprt (S/AFEO), end-of-tour, Lt. Col James E. Betel; Form 4 (S), 7AF DOT to DO, subj: Combat Tactics Activity Report, 23 Oct 67; hist (S), 45th TRS, Jul-Sep 67, p. 6.

8.   Hist (S/NOFORN), 7AF, Jul-Dec 67, I, p. 108; hist (C), 460th TRW, Jul-Dec 67, Hist of Det 1, 45th TRS; hist (S), 45th TRS, Jul-Sep 67, p. 7.

9.   Hist (S/NOFORN), 7AF, Jul-Dec 67, l, p. 107; PACAF Summary (TS/NOFORN), Air Ops SEA, XXXIX, Oct 67, p. 4-4, and XL, Nov 67, p. 4-4; hist (S/NOFORN), 7AF, Jan-Jun 68, III, Pt. 5, D-73.

10.   Atch to ltr (TS), 7AF DOCP, subj: Coordination of History, 17 Mar 68.

11.   Hist (TS/NOFORN/AFEO), PACAF, 1967, I, Pt. 2, p. 369; hist (S), 432d TRW, Oct-Dec 67, p. 5; PACAF Summary (TS/NOFORN/AFEO), Air Ops SEA, XL, Nov 67, pp. 1-10 and 4-3; hist (S/NOFORN), 7AF, Jul-Dec 67, I, p. 41.

12.   Hist (S), 460th TFW, Oct-Dec 67, Hist of Det l, 45th TRS.

13.   Msg (S/NOFORN), 7AF, Doc 36928, 231150Z Dec 67; hist (TS), PACAF, 1967, III, pt. 4; hist (TS/NOFORN/AFEO), PACAF, 1968, I, Pt. 2, p. 214, and III, pt 4, D-73.

14.   PACAF Summary (TS/NOFORN/AFEO), Air Ops SEA, XLII, Jan 68, p. 3-2, Jerry Greene, New York News, 25 January 1970 (26); 7AF WAIS (S/NOFORN), 68-19, 11 May 68; hist (S), 7AF, Jan – Jun 68, Pt. 1, pp. 134-135.

15.   Ltr (S), Hq USAFSS (CCB) to AFCD, et al, subj: Resume of Items Presented to Commander and staff, 31 January 1968.

16.   PACAF Summary (TS/NOFORN), Air Pps SEA, XLIII, Feb 68, pp 4-2 to 4-3; Memo for Record (S), subj: Meeting with General Westmoreland

with Gen. Momyer, 5 Feb 68; hist (S), 460th TRW, Jan-Mar 68, list of Det 1, 45th TRS; 7AF WAIS (S/NOFORN), 68 - 19, 11 May 68, p. 29; Maj. A.W. Thompson and C. William Thorndale, Air Response to the Tet Offensive, 30 Jan - 29 Feb 68 (S) (HQ PACAF, Project CHECO, 12 Aug 68), p. 6

17.   Hist (S/NOFORN), 7AF, Jul-Dec 68, III, pt. 5, Doc. D-102A.

18.   Hist (S/NOFORN), 7AF, Jan-Jun 68, III, pt. 4, D-G4.

19.   Msg (S), 7AF to Dep Comdr, 7/13AF et al, 1 Apr 68; Lyndon Baines Johnson, The Vantage Point, New York, Holt-Rinehart and Winston, 1971, p. 50.

20.   Hist (S), 7AF, Jan-Jun 68, I, pt. 1, pp. 4-5, 147 - 147a.

21.   Hist (S), 460th TRW, Apr-Jun 68, p. v, and App 6, Tabs E, F, and H.

22.   Hist (TS/NOFORN), MACV, 1968, I, p, 220 hist (S/NOFORN), 460th TRW, Apr-Jun 68, p. 27.

23.   Hist (S), 460th TRW, Jul-Sep 68, I, p. 25.

24.   Hist (S/NOFORN), 7AF, Jul-Dec 69, III, pt. 4, Doc. C-3, 10-11; hist (S/NOFORN), 7AF, Jul-Dec 68; I, Pt. 1, p. 240.

25.   Hist (S), 460th TRW, Jul-Sep 68, I, p. 7.

26.   Hist (S), 7AF, Jul-Dec 68, I, pr. 1, p. xxx; hist (S/NOFORN), 460th TRW, Jul-Sep 68, p. 21; rprt (S/AFEO), end-of-tour, Maj. Gen. Gordon F. Blood, Aug 67 - Jan 69, p 46.

27.   Hist (S), 460th TRW, Jul-Sep 68, I, p. 30; ltr (C), 460th TRW DCM to 7AF (D1M), subj: Inspection of RF-101 Aircraft Modified IAW Modification 1181, 26 Jul 68.

28.   Johnson, The Vantage Point, pp. 519, 528.

29.   Hist (S), 460th TRW, Oct - Dec 68, II, App. XVI, p. viii.

30.   Hist (S), 460th TRW, Oct - Dec 68, II, App. XVI, p. 8.

31.   Hist (S), 460th TRW, Jan - Mar 69, II, p. vi.

32.   Msg (S), 7AF to MACV J-3, 040815Z Mar 69; msg (S), CINCPAC to COMUSMACV, 080415 Mar 69; hist (TS/NOFORN), PACAF, Jan-Jun 69, I, pp. 63-64.

33.   Msg (S), 7A.F, DOCT-69-S-0474, 090640Z Feb 69; hist (TS/NOFORN/AFEO), PACAF, Jan-Jun 69, I, p. 110; hist (S/NOFORN), 7AF, Jan-Jun 69, I, Pt. 1, pp. 3-4, 24; hist (S/NOFORN/AFEO), 460th TRW, Jan-Mar 69, I, pp. 19 - 20, and II, App. IX, p. 10.

34.   Hist (S), 460th TRW, Jan - Mar 69, II, p. vii, and Apr - Jun 69, I, pp. 20-21.

35.   Hist (S), 460th TRW, Oct - Dec 69, II, App. 18, p. 5.

36.   Hist (S), 460th TRW, Jul - Sep 69, II, App. 19, p. 9, and Oct - Dec 69, I, p. 33.

37.   Hist (S), 460th TRW, Jul-Sep 69, I, p. 21, and II, App. 19, p. 6.

38.   Hist (S), 460th TRW, Oct - Dec 69, II, App. 14, p. 10.

39.   Hist (S), 460th TRW, Oct - Dec 69, I, p. 9; hist (TS), PACAF, Jul 69-Jun 70, I, pt. 1, p. 21.

40.   Hist (S), 460th TRW, Jan-Mar 70, I, p. 28.

41.   Hist (S), TFA, Jan-Jun 70, I, p. 7; hist (S), 432d TRW, Jan - Mar 70, II, Hist of llth TRS, p. 6; ltr (S); DOCR to 432d TRW, subj: Truck photo Reconnaissance, 13 Jan 70.

42.   Hist (S/NOFORN), 7AF, Jul - Dec 69, I , Pt. 1, p. 178.

43.   Hist (S), 460th TRW, Jan - Mar 70, II, App. 14, p.18, and Apr 70, II, p. 13.

44.   Hist (S), 460th TRW, Jan-Mar 70, II, hist (S), 432d TRW, Jan-Mar 70, II, Hist of llth IRS, p. 5.

45.   Hist (S), 460th TRW, Apr - Jun 70, II, App. 18, p.2, and App. 22, p.15; hist (TS), MACV, TS Supp, 1970, p. TSS-7; Background paper (S) on Tactical Reconnaissance in Cambodia, 1 May 70 - 30 October 70, 7AF/DXR, 8 Nov 70; msg (S), CINCPAC to AIG 7240, 290250Z May 70.

46.   Msg (TS), COMUSMACV to CINCPAC, MAC 6006, 041044Z May 70; 7AF/DOXR Background Paper (S) on Tactical Reconnaissance in Cambodia, 1 May 70 – 30 0ctober 70, 8 Nov 70; DF (S), 7AF DOCRI, 22 May 70.

47.   Maj. D. I. Folkman and Maj. P. D. Caine, The Cambodian campaign , 29 April - 30 June 1970 (TS/NOFORN/AFEO) (HQ PACAF, Project CHECO, 1 Sep 70), p. xvi.

48.   Hist (S) , 460th TRW, Jul-Sep 70, p. 13; hist (TS) PACAF, Jul 69 - Jun 70, I, Pt. 1, pp. 136-137; PACAF Summary (TS/NOFORN), Air Ops SEA, LXXI, Jun 70, pp. 1, 4-2.

49.   Hist (TS), PACAF, Jul 70 - Jun 71, I, pp. 26, 91-92; msg (S), 7AF to MACV (J-3), DOCR-70-0321, 6 Feb 70; Washington Post. 4 Nov 70, p.29; hist (S/NOFORN), 450 TRW, Apr-Jun 70, I. pp. 21-22; msg (s), TAC/USAFSTRIKE to AIG 8094 et al, 031930Z Nov 70; Command Correspondence Staff Summary Sheet (S), DOCR, 3 Feb 70.

GLOSSARY OF TERMS AND ABBREVIATIONS

AAA   Anti-Aircraft Artillery

ABCCC.   Airborne Battlefield Command and Control Center. In SEA, a C-47, C-7, C-130, or other aircraft with special communications equipment manned by staff personnel authorized to control the air battle.

Able Mable   U.S. aerial reconnaissance project in SEA using RF-l0lCs from the 15th and 45th Tactical Reconnaissance Squadrons.

Acoustic   Operated by or utilizing sound waves. The acoustic sensors reacted to and transmitted detonations, voices, truck motors, and similar sounds.

AD   Air Division

ADC   Air Defense Command

ADVON   Advance Echelon

AFEO   Air Force Eyes Only (Security rating)

AFM   Air Force Manual

Afterburner   An auxiliary combustion chamber within, or attached to, the tailpipe of certain jet engines, in which hot unused oxygen of exhaust gases from fuel already burned is used to burn a second fuel and thus augment the temperature and density of the exhaust gases as they leave the tailpipe, with consequent increase in thrust.

AGL   Above Ground Level

AIRA   Air Attaché

All –weather   Usable or serviceable under any condition of weather or visibility.

AMC   Air Material Command

AMEMBASSY   American Embassy

APGC   Air Proving Ground Command

ARDC	Air Research and Development Command
BDA	Bomb Damage Assessment
Blue Tree	Pre-strike reconnaissance over North Vietnam
C	Classified (Security rating)
CHMAAG	Chief Military Assistance Advisory Group
CHECO	Contemporary Historical Examination of Current Operations
CINCPAC	Commander in Chief, Pacific Command
CINCPACAF	Commander in Chief, Pacific Air Forces
CINCPACFLT	Commander in Chief, Pacific Fleet
COIN	Counter-Insurgency
COMUSMACV	Commander, U.S. Military Assistance Command, Vietnam
Crachin	Vietnamese term applied to weather periods with low cloud bases, constant drizzle, occasional heavy rain, and fog.
CSAF	Chief of Staff, United States Air Force
DIA	Defense Intelligence Agency
Dicing	A type of reconnaissance mission flown at very low altitudes to take forward or side oblique photographs. (Defense Lion Note: So called because the pilot is dicing with death from AAA fire).
DMZ	Demilitarized Zone
ECM	Electronic Countermeasures
Exploit	The plotting and interpretation of aerial photography to derive as much as possible of the intelligence contained therein, including enlarging the prints, preparing duplicates or transparencies, and such other manipulation as might be necessary to assist in the interpretation.
Fan array	A camera arrangement of three or more aerial cameras so mounted as to provide a vertical photograph and two or more obliques photographs exposed simultaneously with overlap between each, covering a side-to-side swath from horizon to horizon.
FIELD GOAL	RT-33 reconnaissance over Laos and Thailand.
Focal length	The length or distance separating the camera lens from the film or plate; more technically, the length or distance between the rear nodal point (the point of emergence) of a camera lens and the focal plane.

FY	fiscal year
G	gravity
GPO	Government Printing Office
HF	high frequency
ICC	International Control Commission
IFF	identification, friend or foe
IMC	image motion compensation
IP	initial point
JCS	Joint Chiefs of Staff
JTF	Joint Task Force
knots	nautical miles per hour
MACV	Military Assistance Command, Vietnam
MAIL POUCH	Courier service by former Field Goal RT-33 to deliver photos and reports from Don Muang Airport to Tan Son Nhut Air Base, Vientiane and Clark Air Base.
MAP	Military Assistance Program
Military power	The maximum power or thrust specified-for-an engine by the manufacturer or by the Air Force as allowable in flight under specified operating conditions for periods of 30 minutes duration; normal rated power.
Monsoon.	A periodic wind; also the period of a wind from a particular direction. (Defense Lion Note: Also a period of exceptionally heavy rainfall during said period that can ground aircraft or endanger the safety of those unable to land before the storm starts.
NOFORN	No Foreign Distribution (Security rating)
NVA	North Vietnamese Army (Defense Lion Note: More formally, the People's Liberation Army of Vietnam)
OL	Operating Location
PACAF	Pacific Air Forces
Panhandle	With some imagination, the form of both Laos and North Vietnam can be likened to a handled pot or pan, hence the long "handle" of the pan becomes the panhandle.
PIPE STEM	Task force of four RF-101Cs from the 15th TRS to participate. in an air show at Saigon in October 1961
POL	petroleum, oil and lubricants

PPC	photo processing cell
PPIF	photo processing and interpretation facility
Psi	pounds per square inch
RITS	Reconnaissance Intelligence Technical Squadron
RLAF	Royal Laotian Air Force
RTAF	Royal Thai Air Force
RTAFB	Royal Thai Air Force Base
RTF	Reconnaissance Task Force
RTG	Royal Thai Government
S	Secret (Security rating)
SAC	Strategic Air Command
SAM	surface-to-air missile
Scale (photo)	A proportion between the photo image and the item photographed; the ratio of the lens focal length and the altitude above the ground level at the instant of exposure with the camera level.
sccs	simplified camera control system
SEA	Southeast Asia
SEATO	Southeast Asia Treaty Organization
Seismic	Of, relating to, resembling, or caused by an earthquake.- The seismic sensors thus recorded and transmitted indications of shock waves passing through the earth caused by footsteps vehicle movement, and detonations.
split-vertical	An arrangement of two cameras whose optical axes are offset from vertical to widen the swath of coverage while retaining overlap between the two simultaneously exposed photographs.
TAC	Tactical Air Command
TARC	Tactical Air Reconnaissance Center
Tet	Lunar new year
TFA	Task Force Alpha
TFW	Tactical Fighter Wing
Toy Tiger	Project to modify RF-l01C camera system to provide high-speed cameras for low-altitude reconnaissance and a night photo capability.

Transshipment	(point) A point at which natural or cultural barriers make it necessary to unload passengers and/or freight from one conveyance and load them on another. Examples are transferring loads from trucks to boats, or moving freight from railroad cars of one rail gauge to those using a different gauge.
TRS	Tactical reconnaissance squadron
TRW	Tactical reconnaissance wing
TS	Top Secret (Security rating)
U	Unclassified (Security rating, more precisely lack thereof)
UHF	Ultra-high frequency
USAFE	United States Air Forces in Europe
USAFSS	United States Air Force Security Service
VC-47	A standard C-47 transport aircraft converted by installing a new interior with bunks, tables, seats, and similar comfort features.
VFR	visual flight rules
VNAF	South Vietnamese Air Force
WADC	Wright Air Development Center
WAIS	Weekly Air Intelligence Summary
YANKEE TEAM	Reconnaissance program over Laos, initially by RF-l0lCs and Navy reconnaissance aircraft.

APPENDIX I
VOODOO CHRONOLOGY

12 February 1952 (U)   McDonnell Aircraft Corporation presented proposed specifications for the first RF'-101A.

October l952 (U)   Headquarters, Air Research. and Development Command (ARDC) stated the requirement for a photo reconnaissance version of the F-101A.

August 1953 (U)   McDonnell Aircraft Corporation presented the RF-101A design proposal, but the Air Materiel Command (AMC) and the Wright Air Development Center (WADC) rejected the design because it contained too many experimental components.

13 January 1954 (U)   RF-101A mock-up approved.

July 1955 (S)   First flight of the YRF-101A.

June 1956 (U)   The Air Force redesignated RF-101As numbered 56-162 through 56-321 as RF-101Cs.

22 March 1957 (U)   The Air Force assigned the first RF-101As to a reconnaissance wing at Shaw Air Force Base.

January 1959 (U)   The 15th Tactical Reconnaissance Squadron (TRS), Pacific Air Forces (PACAF) was operational with RF-101Cs.

March 1959 (U)   The 45th TRS, PACAF, was operational with F-101Cs

6 June 1960 (C)   Four Tactical Air Command (TAC) RF-101Cs deployed to Don Muang Airport, Thailand, to photograph 10 large objectives in 2 days for the Royal Thai Government (RTG).

1 March 1961 (S)   Three RF-101Cs from the 15th TRS deployed to Takhli Royal Thai Air Force Base (RTAFB) for Southeast Asia Treaty Organization (SEATO) Exercise Air Bull.

18 October 1961 (C)   The Pipe Stem Task Force RF-101Cs and photo processing cell (PPC) arrived at Tan Son Nhut Air Base.

23 October 1961 (S)   The Pipe Stem RF-101Cs photographed Soviet transport- aircraft parachuting supplies into Tchepon Airfield, Laos.

25 October 1961 (S)   Two RF-101Cs photographing a Soviet airdrop at Tchepone were subjected to antiaircraft fire.

7 November 1961 (S)	Four RF-101Cs arrived at Don Muang Airport Thailand, as the Able Mable Task Force.
18 November 1961 (C)	The Pipe Stem PPC at Tan Son Nhut Air Base was designated Operating Location Number Two (OL-2) for Able Mable.
21 November 1961 (S)	The International Control Commission (ICC) pressed for the removal of the Pipe Stem RF-101Cs, causing the force to return to Kadena Air Base. It left the PPC at Tan Son Nhut Air Base as the Able Mable OL-2.
12 May 1962 (S)	Joint Task Force 116 (JTF-116) was activated in Southeast Asia using the contingency plan for the defense of Laos.
23 May 1962 (S)	The 15th TRS replaced the 45th TRS on Able Mable duty.
May 1962 (S)	RF-101Cs modified under Project Toy Tiger arrived at Kadena Air Base for tests in Southeast Asia.
14 August 1962 (S)	Antiaircraft fire hit and seriously damaged an RF-101C over Route 7 in Laos.
1 September 1962 (S)	The Commander-in-Chief, Pacific authorized limited reconnaissance over Laos.
3 November 1962 (S)	The Toy Tiger RF-101Cs returned to the United States for possible use in the Cuban Missile crisis.
6 November 1962 (S)	The Joint Chiefs of Staff (JCS) terminated all US aerial reconnaissance overflight of Laos.
14 November 1962 (S)	The 45th TRS replaced the 15th TRS on Able Mable duty.
14 December 1962 (S)	The Able Mable Task Force, completed a move from Don Muang Airport, Thailand, to Tan Son Nhut Air Base, South Vietnam.
l April 1963 (S)	The strength of the Able Mable Task Force grew to six RF-101Cs.
1 May 1963 (S)	The 15th TRS replaced the 45th TRS on Able Mable duty.
1 November 1963 (S)	The 45th TRS replaced the 15th TRS on Able Mable duty.
1 May 1964 (C)	The 15th TRS replaced the 45th TRS on Able Mable duty.

17 May 1964 (S)	Pathet Lao forces drove the Neutralist forces from the Plain of Jars to open a new campaign to control all of Laos.
19 May 1964 (S)	Four RF-101Cs flew the first reconnaissance sorties over Laos since December 1962.
22 May 1964 (S)	The JCS assigned the nickname Yankee Team to sorties over Laos.
9 June 1964 (S)	As a reaction to the downing of two Navy aircraft over Laos , the JCS orders strikes on anti-aircraft gun sites at Xieng Khouang.
1 August 1964 (S)	The Able Mable Task Force began scheduling daily weather reconnaissance missions over Laos.
9 August 1964 (S)	Six RF-101Cs of the 20th TRS and two replacement RF-l01Cs arrived at Kadena Air Base.
21 November 1964 (S)	Antiaircraft fire destroyed an RF-l01C over Ban-Phan Nop, the first such loss in Southeast Asia. Rescue aircraft picked up the pilot.
1 February 1965 (S)	The 45th TRS replaced the 15th TRS on Able Mable duty, bringing modified RF-101Cs to Southeast Asia for the first time.
7 February 1965 (S)	Viet Cong attacks on an Army command at Pleiku sparked the first US bombing of North Vietnam.
10 February 1965 (C)	Viet Cong attacks on US billets at Qui-Non resulted in USAF and South Vietnamese Air Force (VMF) air strikes against targets in North Vietnam
18 March 1965 (S)	The JCS issued operations order Blue Tree to formalize daily reconnaissance flights over North Vietnam.
31 March 1965 (S)	Four RF-101Cs from the 15th TRS arrived at Udorn RTAFB to form the Green Python Task Force.
29 April 1965 (S)	The Green Python Task Force lost its first RF-101C The pilot landed safely but was captured.
29 April 1965 (S)	Three RF-101Cs flew the first electronic countermeasures (ECM) mission over North Vietnam in support of a strike mission.
6 May 1965 (S)	Six RF-101Cs of the 363d Tactical Reconnaissance Wing (TRW) from TAC, then on temporary duty at Kadena Air Base, augmented the Green Python Task Force at Udorn RTAFB.

6 November 1965 (S)   The RF-101Cs of the 45th TRS returned to Misawa Air Base, Japan.

11-13 November 1965 (S) The 20th TRS, without aircraft, moved from Shaw Air Force Base to Tan Son Nhut Air Base, where it took over the Able Mable mission. The 15th TRS provided 12 RF-101Cs for the use of the new squadron.

18 February 1966 (S)   PACAF activated the 460th TRW at Tan Son Nhut Air Base.

30 March 1966 (U)   The 20th TRS moved its RF-101Cs from Tan Son Nhut Air Base to Udorn RTAFB to replace the Green Python Task Force.

30 March 1966 (U)   The 45th TRS sent 12 RF-101Cs to Tan Son Nhut Air Base to take over Able Mable duties.

1 April 1966 (U)   PACAF activated Seventh Air Force at Tan Son Nhut Air Base to replace the 2d Air Division.

23 July 1966 (S)   PACAF moved all of the 45th TRS aircraft and personnel to Tan Son Nhut Air Base. as Detachment 1 of that squadron.

18 September 1966 (S)   PACAF activated the 432d TRW at Udorn RTAFB

21 June 1967 (S)   A surface-to-air missile (SAM) destroyed an RF-101C southwest of Hoa Binh, the first loss to a SAM.

28 August 1967 (S)   The 45th TRS deployed a photo processing and interpretation facility (PPIF) to Phu Cat Air Base to support reconnaissance missions over northern South Vietnam.

16 September 1967 (S)   Seventh Air Force prohibited RF-101C sorties over northern North Vietnam

31 October 1967 (S)   PACAF deactivated the 20th TRS at Udorn RTAFB and transferred its personnel and RF-101Cs to Tan Son Nhut Air Base.

31 March 1968 (U)   President Johnson halted all bombardment of North Vietnam above the panhandle. Reconnaissance continued.

31 October 1968 (U)   President Johnson halted bombardment of North Vietnam. Reconnaissance continued.

28 October 1969 (S)   Forward operating Location (FoL) at Phu Cat Air Base closed and personnel and equipment returned to Tan Son Nhut Air Base

110

6 May 1970 (S)   The JCS authorized tactical aerial reconnaissance over Cambodia to a depth of 60 nautical miles.

1 November 1970 (S)   Det 1, 45th TRS, halted all reconnaissance operations preparatory to inactivation.

16 November 1970 (S)   The last RF-101C left Tan Son Nhut for the U.S.

APPENDIX II
AIRCRAFT DESCRIPTION

The Taiwanese Air Force was the only known foreign operator of the RF-101 Voodoo.

Source: U.S. Air Force.

Description

The RF-101 (A&C) is a single-seat, twin-jet fighter aircraft (McDonnell) of sweptback wing and tail design. It is powered by two J57-P-13 Pratt and Whitney engines, rated at 15,000-pounds thrust with afterburner in operation. The "C" series differs from the "A" only in the internal structure, which has been strengthened to allow maneuver load factors up to 7.33 Gs. The aircraft is equipped with the Simplified-Universal Camera Control System (SUCCS), and has three camera bays (one each for split-vertical, forward oblique, and tri metrogon installations). The cockpit is provided with an ejection seat, 5.0 psi differential pressurization, pressure suit provisions, a liquid oxygen system and a jettisonable canopy.

Special features include speed brakes, power-operated (hydraulic) irreversible flight controls, all-movable stabilizer, MB-1 autopilot, in-flight refueling provisions (both probe-drogue - and flying boom methods single-point ground refueling and a drag parachute.

Characteristics Summary

RECONNAISSANCE RF-101A

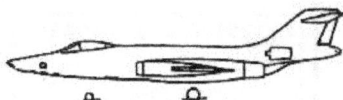

"VOODOO"

McDONNELL

Wing Area . . . . .368.0 sq ft   Length . . . . 69.3 ft

Span . . . . .39.7 ft   Height . . . . .18.0 ft

AVAILABILITY

Number available

ACTIVE	RESERVE	TOTAL

PROCUREMENT

Number to be delivered in fiscal years

STATUS

1. Contract Date: Jan 53

2. Mock-Up: Jan 54

Navy Equivalent: None

3. First Flight: (YRF-101A): May 55
4. First Flight (RF-101A): Jun 56
5. Production Completed

Mfr's Model: 36X

POWER PLANT

(2) J57-P-13

Pratt & Whitney

ENGINE RATINGS

SLS	LB - †RPM - MIN
Max:	*15,000-6150/9900 - 5
Mil:	10,200-6150/9900 - 30
Nor:	8700 -5900/9650 - Cont

*With afterburner operating
†First figure represents RPM of the low pressure spool while the second is that of the high pressure spool.

FEATURES

Crew 1

In-flight refueling provisions

Liquid oxygen system

MB-1 Auto-pilot

Leading & Trailing edge flaps

All-movable stabilizer

Simplified camera control System (SUCCS)

Drag chute

Speed brakes

Max fuel cap: 3150 gal

ARMAMENT

Nr	Type	Lens
HIGH & LOW ALT. DAY MISSION		
1 . . .	KA-2	12"
2 . . .	KA-1	36"
3 . . .	KA-2	6"

113

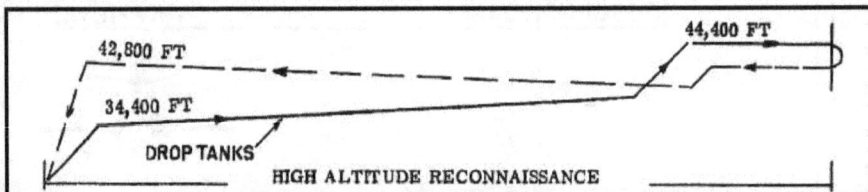

Characteristics Summary Basic Mission RF-101A

44,400 FT

42,800 FT

34,400 FT

DROP TANKS

HIGH ALTITUDE RECONNAISSANCE

PERFORMANCE

COMBAT RADIUS	FERRY RANGE	S P E E D
(b) 9 0 9 naut. mi with 656 lb payload at 478 knots avg. in 3.82 hours.	2 1 1 6 naut. mi with 3600 gal fuel at 478 knots avg. in 4.44 hours at 50,415 lb T.O. wt.	COMBAT 768 knots at 44,400 ft alt, max power MAX 876 knots at 35,000 ft alt, max power BASIC 876 knots at 35,000 ft alt, max power

C L I M B	C E I L I N G	TAKE-OFF
8480 fpm sea level, take-off weight military power	39,200 ft 100 fpm, take-off weight military power	(b) ground run 5430 ft | ——— ft no assist | assisted
37,500 fpm sea level, combat weight maximum power	51,450 ft 500 fpm, combat weight maximum power	over 50 ft height (b) 9180 ft | ——— ft no assist | assisted

L O A D	W E I G H T S	STALLING SPEED
Photo Equipment . . . 656 lb Fuel: 3150 gal protected 13.6 % droppable 28.6 % external 28.6 %	Empty..... 25,335 lb Combat... 35,751 lb Take-off 47,331 lb limited by mission	172 knots power-off, landing config- uration, take-off weight **TIME TO CLIMB** 3.4 min S.L. to 35,000 ft, take-off weight, military power

N O T E S

1. Performance Basis:
   (a) Phase IV flight test data.
   (b) With military power; by using afterburner (max power) take-off values are 3270 ft
     and 4450 ft and the radius is reduced to 866 nautical miles.

2. Revision Basis:
   To reflect changes in combat ceiling and stall speed.

Standard Aircraft Characteristics

RF-101C

VOODOO

McDonnell

TWO J57-P-13

PRATT & WHITNEY

BY AUTHORITY OF
THE SECRETARY
OF THE AIR FORCE

Note: The Second Page of this Standard Aircraft Characteristics document can be found on page 18 maintaining the layout of the original monograph.

Loading and Performance — Typical Mission

CONDITIONS	(units)	BASIC MISSION I	DESIGN MISSION II	HIGH LOW HIGH III	LOW HIGH IV	LOW LOW LOW V	HIGH ALT. REFUEL VI	FERRY RANGE VII
TAKE-OFF WEIGHT	(lb)	48,133	48,133	48,133	48,133	48,133	48,133	48,083
Fuel at 6.5 lb/gal (grade JP-4)	(lb)	20,475	20,475	20,475	20,475	20,475	20,475	20,475
Payload (Photo Equip)	(lb)	652	652	652	652	652	652	652
Wing loading	(lb/sq ft)	130.8	130.8	130.8	130.8	130.8	130.8	130.7
Stall speed (power off)	(kn)	172	172	172	172	172	172	172
Take-off ground run at SL	(ft)	3380/5650	3380/5650	3380/5650	3380/5650	3380/5650	3380/5650	3375/5630
Take-off to clear 50 ft	(ft)	4630/9710	4630/9710	4630/9710	4630/9710	4630/9710	4630/9710	4630/9680
Rate of climb at SL	(fpm)	8300	8300	8300	8300	8300	8300	8310
Time: SL to 20,000 ft	(min)	3.21	3.21	3.21	3.21	3.21	3.21	3.20
Time: SL to 30,000 ft	(min)	5.50	5.50	5.50	5.50	5.50	5.50	5.50
Service ceiling (100 fpm)	(ft)	38,900	38,900	38,900	38,900	38,900	38,900	38,900
COMBAT RANGE	(n mi)	888 ⑧	897					1864
COMBAT RADIUS	(n mi)			745	571	457	1422	
Average cruise speed	(kn)	479	479	478	430	374	477	478
Initial cruising altitude	(ft)	34,100	34,100	34,100	5000	5000	34,100	34,100
Target speed	(kn)	509	506	595	595	595	510	
Target altitude	(ft)	44,000	44,100	S.L.	S.L.	S.L.	41,400	
Final cruising altitude	(ft)	42,100	42,100	42,100	42,100	5000	42,100	42,200
Total mission time	(hr)	3.73	3.73	3.08	2.58	2.34	5.97	3.90
Refueling altitude	(ft)						38,600/32,900	
Refuel distance from target outbound	(n mi)						525	
Fuel added outbound	(lb)						11,388	
COMBAT WEIGHT	(lb)	36,586	36,554	37,022	35,657	37,483	41,357	29,529
Combat altitude	(ft)	44,000	44,100	S.L.	S.L.	S.L.	41,400	42,200
Combat speed	(kn)	768	765	637	637	637	784	843
Combat climb	(fpm)	6070	6010	36,150	37,600	35,650	6280	11,140
Combat ceiling (500 fpm)	(ft)	50,600	50,600	50,400	51,100	50,100	48,200	54,800
Service ceiling (100 fpm)	(ft)	45,200	45,200	45,000	45,800	44,800	42,800	49,600
Max rate of climb at SL	(fpm)	36,600	36,650	36,150	37,600	35,650	32,100	45,550
Basic speed at 35,000 ft	(kn)	875	875	875	876	875	871	879
LANDING WEIGHT	(lb)	29,579	29,579	29,579	29,579	29,579	29,579	29,529
Ground roll at SL	(ft)	4225	4225	4225	4225	4225	4225	4220
Ground roll (auxiliary brake)	(ft)	2950	2950	2950	2950	2950	2950	2940
Total from 50 ft	(ft)	5525	5525	5525	5525	5525	5525	5510
Total from 50 ft (auxiliary brake)	(ft)	4230	4230	4230	4230	4230	4230	4220

NOTES:
① Max power
② Military power
③ Normal power
④ Detailed description of RADIUS and RANGE
⑤ Speed brakes extended
⑥ Using 15.6 ft drag chute
⑦ Fuel loads defined on page 6
⑧ By using afterburner for take-off
⑨ Recommended minimum speed

PERFORMANCE BASIS:
(a) Data source: Based on Phase IV flight tests
(b) Performance is based on powers shown on page 3

POWER PLANT

Nr & Model	(2) J57-P-13
Mfr	Pratt & Whitney
Engine Spec. Nr	A-1688D
Type	Axial
Length	211.0"
Diameter	40.3"
Weight (Dry)	5025 lb
Tail Pipe	Two-Position
Augmentation	Afterburning

ENGINE RATINGS

S. L. Static LB -	RPM	- MIN
Max	*15,000 - 6150/3900	- 5
Mil	10,200 - 6150/3900	- 30
Nor	8700 - 5900/3650	- Cont

*With afterburner operating

First figure represents the RPM of the low pressure spool while the second that of the high pressure spool.

DIMENSIONS

Wing	
Span	39.7'
Incidence (root)	1°
(tip)	1°
Dihedral	0°
Sweepback (25% chord)	36°36'
Length	69.3'
Height	18.0'
Tread	19.9'

Mission and Description

Navy Equivalent: None   Mfrs Model: 36X

The principal mission of the RF-101C is long range high and low altitude reconnaissance.

Cameras and related equipment are located in the nose and forward portion of the fuselage and are readily accessible from the ground. A photographic, navigation viewfinder and velocity-altitude comparator, with drift and wide angle optical objective systems, is provided. The Simplified Universal Camera Control System (SUCCs) is provided for camera control.

Special features of this aircraft include swept-back wing and tail, hydraulic power-operated irreversible flight controls all movable stabilizer, anti-fatigue autopilot (MB-1) and in-flight refueling provisions (both the Probe-Drogue and Flying Boom method). Speed brakes are provided for rapid deceleration and a drag chute for assistance in stopping after landing. The cockpit is provided with ejection seat. 5.0 PSI differential pressurization, pressure suit provisions. liquid oxygen system, and a jettisonable canopy.

Development

Same as the RF-101A except for strengthening of the internal structure thereby allowing the maneuvering load factor to be increased to 7.33 g.

Contract date	Mar 56
First flight	Sep 57
First acceptance	Sep 57
Production status	In Production

GUNS

NONE

CAMERAS

Nr	Station	Type	Lens
HIGH & LOW ALT. DAY MISSION			
1	Fwd Firing	KA-2	12"
2	Split Vert	KA-1	36"
3	Tri-Metrogon	KA-2	6"

WEIGHTS

Loading	LB	L.F.
Empty	26,136(E)	
Basic	28,271 (E)	
Design	37,000	6.33
Combat	36,386	
Max T.O.	‡51,000	
Max Land	†44,000	

(E) Estimated
◊ For basic mission
‡ Limited by landing gear strength
† Maximum design landing weight

FUEL

Location	Nr Tanks	Gal
Fuselage	5	2079
Wing	8	171
Fus. Ext. Drop	2	900
	† Total	3150
Grade		JP-4
Specification		MIL-F-5624A

OIL

Eng. Integral	(tot) 600
Specification	MIL-L-7808
* Self-Sealing (430 gal sump tank only)	

† See fuel loading page 6

ELECTRONICS

UHF Command	AN/ARC-34
Omni-Directional	
Recv'r	AN/ARN-14D
Direction Finder	AN/ARA-25
IFF	AN/APX-6A
Ground Position	
Indicator	AN/ASN-6
Radar Altimeter	AN/APN-22
Radar Warning	AN/APS-54
Intercommunication	AN/AIC-10

117

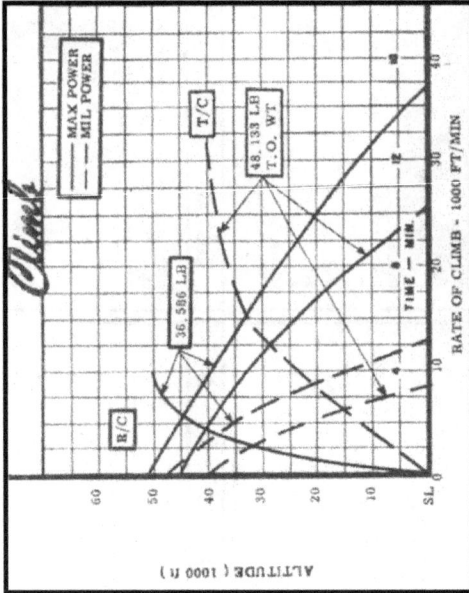

Climb

MAX POWER
MIL POWER

48,133 LB
T.O. WT.

36,586 LB

T/C

R/C

RATE OF CLIMB - 1000 FT/MIN

TIME ~ MIN.

ALTITUDE (1000 ft)

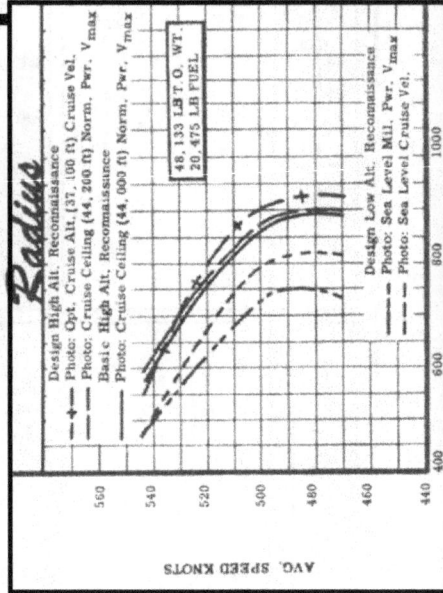

Radius

Design High Alt. Reconnaissance
Photo: Opt. Cruise Alt. (37, 100 ft) Cruise Vel.
Photo: Cruise Ceiling (44, 200 ft) Norm. Pwr. Vmax
Basic High Alt. Reconnaissance
Photo: Cruise Ceiling (44, 000 ft) Norm. Pwr. Vmax

Design Low Alt. Reconnaissance
Photo: Sea Level Mil. Pwr. Vmax
Photo: Sea Level Cruise Vel.

48,133 LB T.O. WT.
20,475 LB FUEL

AVG. SPEED KNOTS

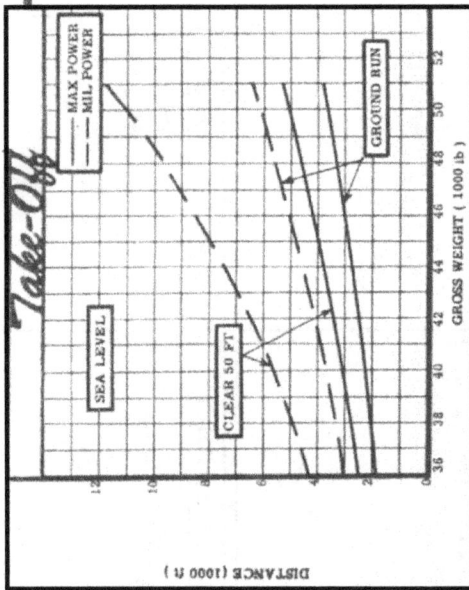

Take-Off

MAX POWER
MIL POWER

GROUND RUN

SEA LEVEL

CLEAR 50 FT

GROSS WEIGHT (1000 lb)

DISTANCE (1000 ft)

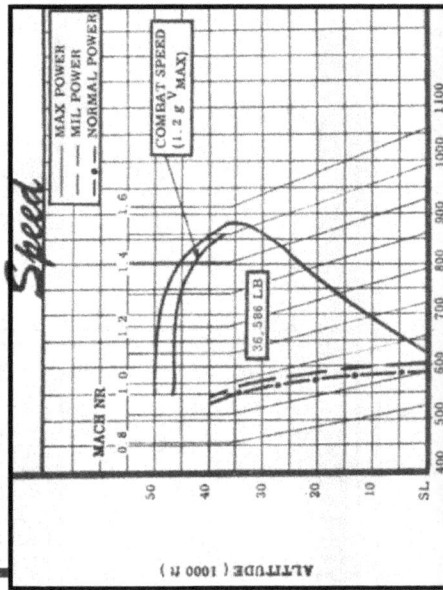

Speed

MAX POWER
MIL POWER
NORMAL POWER

COMBAT SPEED
(1.2 g Vmax)

36,586 LB

MACH NR.

ALTITUDE (1000 ft)

N O T E S

FORMULA: RADIUS MISSION I

Take-off with military power, climb on course with military power to initial cruise altitude, cruise at cruise altitude at maximum range speeds, climb on course with military power to cruise ceiling, conduct a 15 minute normal power reconnaissance strip run, allow 2 minutes for normal power evasive action, and conduct an 8 minute normal power escape, cruise back to base at cruise altitude at maximum range speed. Range free allowances include 5 minutes at normal power at sea level for starting engines and take-off 2 minutes of combat with normal power at cruise ceiling and a reserve of 20 minutes loiter at sea level at speeds for maximum endurance (two engines) and 5% of initial fuel load.

FORMULA: RADIUS MISSION II

Take-off with military power, climb on course with military power to initial cruise altitude, cruise at cruise altitude at maximum range speeds, climb on course with military power to cruise ceiling conduct a 100 nautical mile, normal power reconnaissance strip run, conduct a 100 nautical mile, normal power run-out, cruise back to base at cruise altitude at maximum range speeds. Range free allowances include 5 minutes at normal power at sea level for starting engines and take-off and a reserve of 20 minutes loiter at sea level at speeds for maximum endurance (two engines) and 5% of initial fuel load.

FORMULA: RADIUS MISSION III

Take-off with military power, climb on course with military power to initial cruise altitude, cruise at cruise altitude at maximum range speeds, descend to sea level, conduct a 50 nautical mile, military power recon- naissance strip run, conduct a 50 nautical mile, military power run-out, climb on course with military power to initial cruise home altitude, cruise back to base at cruise altitude at maximum range speeds. Range free al- lowances include 5 minutes at normal power at sea level for starting en- gines and take-off and a reserve of 20 minutes loiter at sea level at speeds for maximum endurance (two engines) and 5% of initial fuel load.

FORMULA: RADIUS MISSION IV

Take-off with military power, climb on course with military power to 5000 feet, cruise out at 5000 feet at maximum range speeds, descend to sea level, conduct a 50 nautical mile, military power reconnaissance strip run, conduct a 50 nautical mile, military power run out, climb on course with military power to initial cruise home altitude, cruise back to base at cruise altitude at maximum range speeds. Range free allowances include 5 minutes at normal power at sea level for starting engines and take-off, and a reserve of 20 minutes loiter at sea level for speeds for maximum endurance (two engines) and 5% of initial fuel load.

FORMULA: RADIUS MISSION V

Take-off with military power, climb on course with military power to 5000 feet, cruise out at 5000 feet at maximum range speeds, descend to sea level, conduct a 50 nautical mile, military power reconnaissance strip run, conduct a 50 nautical mile, military power run out, climb on course with military power to 5000 feet, cruise back to base at 5000 feet at maximum range speeds. Range free allowances include 5 minutes at normal power at sea level for starting engines and take-off, and a reserve of 20 minutes loiter at sea level at speeds for maximum endurance (two engines) and 5% of initial fuel load.

FORMULA: RADIUS MISSION VI

Same as Mission I except refuel at outbound point of no return. Fuel and distance allowances are made for period of fuel transfer.

FORMULA: RANGE MISSION VII

Take-off with military power, climb on course with military power to initial cruise altitude, cruise at cruise altitude at maximum range speeds, to remote base. Range free allowances include 5 minutes at normal power at sea level for starting engines and take-off, and a reserve of 20 minutes loiter at sea level at speeds for maximum endurance (two engines) and 5% of initial fuel load.

GENERAL NOTES:

(a) 2-450 gal. tank configuration: tanks are dropped simultaneously when both are empty unless otherwise specified.

PERFORMANCE REFERENCE:

(a) McDonnell Report Nr 5447, Model F-101A/C and RF-101A/C Performance Data Substantiation Report", 15 June 1957.

REVISION BASIS:

Data recoordinated.

FUEL LOADINGS - MISSIONS I, II, III, IV, V, VI, & VII

Fuel load includes 900 gal of external fuel (2-450 gal tanks). Internal cap- acity is limited by inflight refuel boom receptacle to 2230 gal and includes 171 gal of integral wing fuel. Radius is reduced approximately 51 nautical miles if integral wing fuel is not carried.

APPENDIX III
RF-101C LOSSES IN SOUTHEAST ASIA

21 November 1964   Ground fire downed an RF-101C near Ban Phan Nop, Laos. The pilot was rescued.

13 January 1965   Enemy antiaircraft fire downed an RF-101C.

3 April 1965   Enemy antiaircraft fire downed an RF-101C. The pilot returned to US control with the POWS in 1973.

29 April 1965   Enemy antiaircraft fire downed an RF-101C near Sam Neua. Laos. The pilot was listed as missing in action.

6 May 1961   Automatic weapons fire downed an RF-101C on a mission over North Vietnam. No parachute was seen.

22 May 1965   Mechanical failure caused an RF-101C to crash on landing at Ubon RTAFB. The aircraft was destroyed but the pilot was uninjured.

29 June 1965   Enemy antiaircraft fire downed an RF-101C over the Son Tay Army Barracks, 140 miles northwest of Hanoi. The pilot was listed as missing in action.

29 July 1965   Ground fire hit an RF-101C near Phu Tho, causing it to explode. The pilot was killed in action.

13 August 1965   Antiaircraft fire downed an RF-101C between Phu Tho and Viet Tri. The pilot was listed as missing in action.

27 September 1965   Intense automatic weapons fire hit RF-101C 56-204 approximately 27 nautical miles north of Thanh Hoa. The aircraft caught fire and broke up. The pilot was listed as missing in action.

17 October 1965   Antiaircraft fire heavily damaged RF101C 56-178 near Yan Bai. The aircraft was destroyed on landing, the pilot was injured slightly.

1 November 1965   Antiaircraft fire hit RF-101C #56-174 while it was at 500 feet and high speed southwest of Hanoi and caused it to crash. The pilot was listed as missing in action.

26 January 1966   Ground fire hit an RF-101C over the Kuan Son Barracks in North Vietnam. The pilot was returned with the other POWs in 1973.

7 March 1966   Two RF-101Cs on a mission to an area 30 nautical miles north of Vinh disappeared without a trace. The two pilots are listed as killed in action. (SAMs suspected)

21 March 1966	Ground fire hit and set afire RF-101C 56-066 while it was flying along Route 1 between Vinh and Thanh Hoa. The pilot was returned with the POWs.
3 April 1966	Ground fire hit RF-101C 56-172 over North Vietnam. The pilot ejected and was captured. He returned. to US control with the POWs in 1973.
22 April 1966	An RF-101C apparently was hit by ground fire over the Cao Nung Railroad bridge and the pilot ejected. He was a POW until 1973.
6 July 1966	RF-101C 56-051 failed to return from a mission over northern North Vietnam. The captured pilot was a POW until 1973.
31 July 1966	RF-101C 56-226 failed to return from a mission in the Hanoi area. The pilot was captured and released in 1973 with the other POWs.
7 August 1966	On a low-altitude mission in poor weather over western North Vietnam, the pilot of RF-101 56-064 flew into the ground, but the aircraft bounced high enough for him to eject. He was rescued.
12 August 1966	RF-101C 56-056 disappeared while on a mission in the Hanoi area. The pilot was listed as missing in action.
4 November 1966	Ground fire hit RF-101C 56-175 while it was flying over the DMZ. The pilot ejected over the water of the Gulf of Tonkin and was rescued.
5 December 1966	Ground fire hit RF-101C 56-165 over North Vietnam. The pilot ejected and was in radio contact, but rescue was impossible. The pilot was listed as missing in action.
8 February 1967	Antiaircraft fire hit RF-101C 56-203 over the lower panhandle of North Vietnam, setting it afire. The pilot ejected over the Gulf of Tonkin and a Navy destroyer picked him up.
20 May 1967	While on a mission in the Hanoi area the pilot of RF-101C 56-120 reported that he had been hit. No further contact was made and the aircraft failed to return. The pilot was listed as missing in action.
21 June 1967	RF1-10C 56-085 caught fire and began to come apart after being hit by antiaircraft fire near Hanoi. The pilot ejected and was rescued.

7 July 1967	RF-101C 56-096 lost both engines shortly after take off from Tan Son Nhut Air Base and crashed. The pilot ejected and landed with only minor injuries.
26 July 1967	Mechanical failure caused RF-101C 56-049 to crash. The pilot was uninjured.
1 August 1967	A surface-to-air missile hit RF-101C 56-207 while it was on a mission in the Hanoi area. The pilot did not eject, and was listed as missing in action.
9 August 1967	RF-101C 56-225 collided with an Army UH-1D helicopter over South Vietnam. The pilot ejected and landed with minor injuries.
16 September 1967	A MiG downed RF-101C 56-180 over North Vietnam. The pilot ejected, landed safely, and was captured. He was repatriated in 1973.
18 October 1967	The pilot of RF-101C 56-212 lost the control system at a very low altitude over Laos. He ejected and was rescued several hours over later.
18 February 1968	Enemy rockets and mortar rounds destroyed RF-101C 56-182 on the ground at Tan Son Nhut Air Base.
6 August 1968	Automatic weapons fire hit RF-101C 56-215 over the lower panhandle of North Vietnam. After losing all control of the aircraft, the pilot ejected over the Gulf of Tonkin and was rescued.

www.ingramcontent.com/pod-product-compliance
Lightning Source LLC
La Vergne TN
LVHW091155080426
835509LV00006B/701